Contents

ANDREW BOYD

An Atlas of World Affairs 7th ed

SEVENTH EDITION

METHUEN

LONDON AND NEW YORK

First published in 1957 by
Methuen & Co. Ltd
11 New Fetter Lane
London EC4P 4EE
Second edition, revised, 1959
Third edition, revised, 1960
Reprinted 1961
Fourth edition, revised, 1962
Reprinted three times
Fifth edition, revised, 1964
First published as a University
Paperback (Fifth edition) 1964
Reprinted 1964, 1965 and 1966
Sixth edition, revised and reset, 1970
Seventh edition, revised and reset, 1983

Published in the USA by
Methuen & Co.
in association with Methuen, Inc.
733 Third Avenue, New York
NY 10017

Printed in Great Britain at the
University Press, Cambridge

*British Library Cataloguing in Publication
Data*
Boyd, Andrew
    An atlas of world affairs. – 7th ed.
    1. Geography, Historical – Maps
    I. Title
    911   G1030

    ISBN 0-416-32370-7
    ISBN 0-416-32380-4 Pbk

*Library of Congress Cataloging in
Publication Data*
Boyd, Andrew, 1920–
    An atlas of world affairs.

    Includes index.
    1. World politics – 1945–   – Maps.
    2. Geography, Historical – Maps.
    I. Title.
    G1046.F6B914 1983   911   83-675921
    ISBN 0-416-32370-7 (cased)
    ISBN 0-416-32380-4 (pbk.)

Notes

An italic numeral in brackets – e.g. *(44)* – is a cross-reference. The number refers to a map and its accompanying note, not to a page. So do the entries in the index.

Distances are expressed in this book in miles. One mile is equivalent to approximately 1.61 km. One nautical mile is equivalent to approximately 1.85 km. To convert square miles into square km multiply by 2.59. The tonne and the ton are roughly equivalent.

1 People

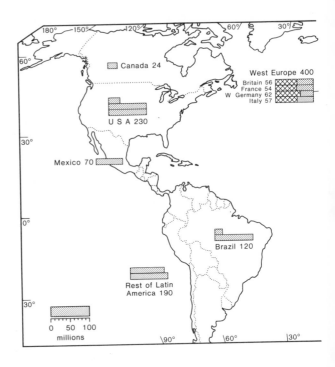

The human race has more than doubled its numbers in the past half century. In 1930 there were about 2000 million people. Now there are about 4600 million. The number added each year is greater than the whole population of Britain or France. By the year 2000 there will probably be well over 6000 million people.

The two biggest masses of people – in China, and in the group made up by India, Pakistan and Bangladesh – are both in Asia. Asia has probably always contained more than half of the human race. Asia and Africa together contain about two-thirds of it. Adding Latin America to them and subtracting Japan, the 'third-world' countries (7) contain about three-quarters. And this proportion is rising, because third-world rates of population growth are relatively high – in spite of the effects in many areas of tropical diseases, recurrent food shortages and even famines. By contrast, in some European countries population growth has virtually ceased.

Growing at 2% a year, a population doubles in 35 years; at $3\frac{1}{2}\%$ it doubles in 20 years. Many third-world countries' populations grew at annual rates between 2% and $3\frac{1}{2}\%$ in the 1970s. In some countries the

6

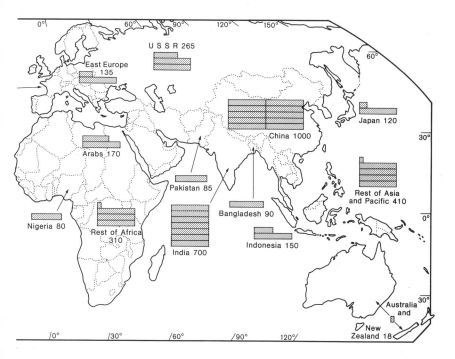

standard of living fell even though the total national income was rising. More people also meant more pressure on natural resources: deforestation, soil erosion, overgrazing, the enlargement of deserts; at sea, overfishing; in fast growing cities, the multiplication of crowded slums.

By the end of the 1970s more than half of the world's countries had adopted policies aimed at reducing birthrates or at least checking their growth. But the results varied widely. Some governments, and some churches, discouraged the limitation of family sizes. In the USSR and Argentina the authorities actively encouraged the raising of large families as contributions to national greatness.

2 Power

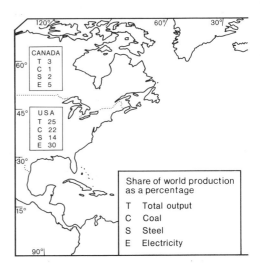

Share of world production as a percentage

T	Total output
C	Coal
S	Steel
E	Electricity

CANADA
T 3
C 1
S 2
E 5

USA
T 25
C 22
S 14
E 30

Three-quarters of the world's total output – and about three-quarters of its coal, steel and electricity – is produced by the USA, USSR, Japan, Canada, the EEC member countries (*19*) and China. Excluding China, this group has only a fifth of the world's population but produces two-thirds of its total output.

Although oil and nuclear energy (*3, 4*) may make more headlines, steel and coal are still important pointers to the distribution of economic power. The 1970s saw steel output falling off in the USA and western Europe – partly because of more output in third-world countries (*5, 7*), partly because of recession linked with oil price rises (*3*). But those same price rises began to spur on coal output in many places.

The major west European countries cannot, as separate states, come anywhere near matching American or Soviet economic power; but their combination in the EEC makes up an entity more comparable with the USA or the USSR.

The most striking recent advance has been that of Japan. It has to import nearly all its oil, coal and iron ore, and its population is only half that of the USA or the USSR, but it has achieved the world's third biggest national output and has raised its living standards to a 'western' level.

A list of all the countries whose economic power gives them international influence would include some major oil exporters. The

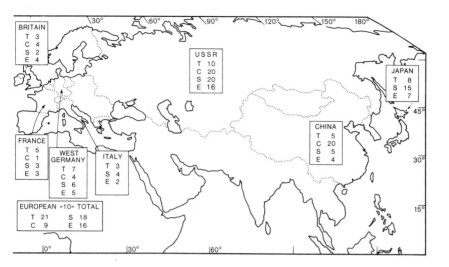

influence of some Arab states in particular has been increased by their oil output (*40*). But, although 60% of the world's known reserves of oil are in the Middle East and North Africa, 42% of its reserves of coal are in North America and western Europe and 40% in the communist countries.

3 Oil

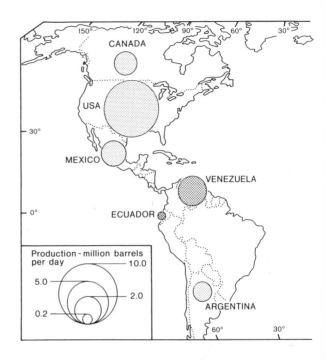

Production - million barrels per day
10.0
5.0
2.0
0.2

In the 1960s coal was replaced, as the world's biggest source of industrial energy, by oil (petroleum) and the natural gas that is often found with it under the earth. World production of crude oil, which had been 275 million tons in 1938, rose to 1050 million tons in 1960, to 2275 million in 1970 and to 3100 million in 1979.

The upsurge was then checked. Between 1979 and 1981 oil output fell by 10%. This was a reaction to the startling increases in oil prices during the 1970s. Prices were roughly tripled in 1973–74 and tripled again in 1978–80. In both cases the rises were linked to turbulence in the Middle East. The effects were most acutely painful for those third-world (7) countries that produced no oil; but inflation and recession hit even the richest industrial states. Total demand for energy stopped growing in many places and even fell in some. Where they could, consumers switched from oil to other sources of energy.

Before the crisis years, the pattern of world production had been changing rapidly. In 1960 a third of all oil output was in the USA; 14% each in the USSR and Venezuela; only a quarter in the Middle East and North Africa. But Middle East oil was easy to extract and thus cheap, and

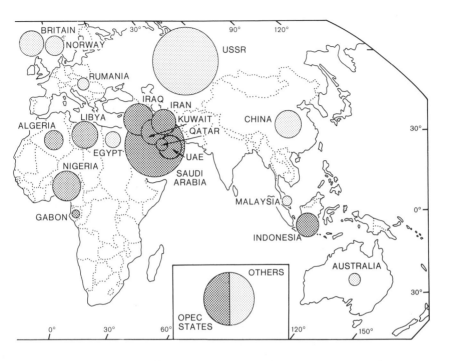

two-thirds of all the reserves then known were in that region. By 1970 the output figures were: Middle East and North Africa 40%, USA 21%, USSR 16%, Venezuela 9%, elsewhere 14%. The Americans were uneasily, the Europeans disturbingly, dependent on imported oil of which the greater part came from Arab states and Iran.

During the 1960s the Organization of Petroleum Exporting Countries (OPEC) was formed (members, in 1982: Algeria, Ecuador, Gabon, Indonesia, Iran, Iraq, Kuwait, Libya, Nigeria, Qatar, Saudi Arabia, United Arab Emirates, Venezuela), and the OPEC states began to try to unite in raising prices. The strength of this 'cartel' was suddenly increased by the Arab–Israeli war in 1973 (*43*), when Arab states cut oil sales to some western countries for a time. Prices soared; national economies sagged – except in the oil-exporting states. The second big wave of price rises began in 1978 when Iran's exports were sharply reduced during the last months of the Shah's rule (*47*). But by 1981, although exports from Iran and Iraq were then affected by the war between them (*48*), the market was shrinking and prices began to fall.

The OPEC states' price increases had spurred on oil exploration and production in many other countries, including Russia. The new fields in the North Sea (22) made Britain virtually self-sufficient in oil by 1980, and provided Norway with a large surplus for export. Mexico became a new major exporter. Australia, Egypt, India and Malaysia made big production increases. So by 1982 the OPEC states were no longer dominating the market as they had done in the early 1970s. However, Saudi Arabia and some of its neighbours (40) still had enormous proved reserves of oil that could be extracted cheaply, whereas much of the new non-OPEC production involved the high costs and high risks of operating in deep waters or in Arctic regions such as Alaska (11, 22, 67).

Lesser oil producers include Angola, Bahrain, Bolivia, Brazil, Brunei, Burma, Chile, Colombia, Oman, Peru, Syria, Trinidad and Tunisia. South Africa has undertaken large-scale production of oil from coal.

Natural gas has in recent years provided the world with an amount of energy roughly equal to half that of all the oil produced. Holland, Italy, New Zealand and Pakistan are among the countries whose gas fields are of special importance to them because they have little or no oil. Until the 1960s nearly all the gas used was moved only through pipelines and, apart from deliveries from Canada to the USA, it was mainly distributed within the countries where it was found. Today, special tankers carry liquefied natural gas (LNG) across the sea; and pipelines from the USSR carry gas to countries in both eastern and western Europe.

4 Nuclear geography

In 1956, at Calder Hall near Windscale in Cumbria, the world's first commercial-scale nuclear reactor began to contribute to Britain's electricity supplies. Nuclear power plants are now operating or being built in most of the industrialized countries (including those under Soviet control) and in several third-world ones (7). So far, they have been producing less than a tenth of the world's electricity, but the proportion is already a third or more in some countries, e.g. France, Sweden and Switzerland. In several western countries sharp controversy has arisen over proposals to use more nuclear energy; oil price rises (3) and fears about the exhaustion of reserves of oil and coal, and about pollution, have encouraged decisions to use it; alarm about the risks involved has worked the other way. Much still depends on solving the problem of disposing of dangerous reactor waste.

All the nuclear power hitherto produced has come from uranium (there are possibilities of supplementing it with thorium). A ton of natural uranium can produce more energy than 10,000 tons of coal. That figure may eventually be multiplied many times by the development of 'breeder' reactors.

Uranium has been found in many countries, but it is often thinly dispersed and costly to extract. Although Sweden has huge reserves it has found it cheaper to import fuel for its reactors; and much of South Africa's uranium has been extractable at a competitive price only because it was a by-product of goldmining. The biggest known reserves of richer uranium ores are in Australia, Canada, Niger and the USA. During the 1970s the biggest recorded production was in the USA, Canada, South Africa, France and Niger, in that order. (China and Russia mine uranium, but keep their figures for production and reserves secret.)

Fear that wider use of nuclear energy might bring wider access to nuclear weapons helped to produce the 1968 Nuclear Non-Proliferation Treaty (NPT), aimed at limiting that access to the five countries which already had these weapons. Three of the five (USA, USSR, Britain) undertook not to help other states to acquire nuclear arms; the other NPT states (112 by 1982) agreed that the International Atomic Energy Agency (IAEA) should inspect all their nuclear installations, affix seals, and see

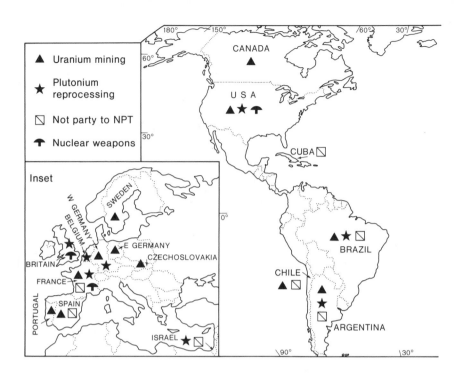

that no material was diverted for making weapons. But nuclear-armed China and France refused to sign the treaty; and the other non-signatories include several states that are thought to be close to an ability to make nuclear weapons. These non-NPT 'near-nuclear' states include Argentina, Brazil, India, Israel, Pakistan and South Africa. In 1974 India staged a nuclear test explosion. Its claims that it had only peaceful purposes in mind were received with suspicion, and after 1974 India found it more difficult to obtain some of the supplies that its nuclear development plans required.

An atomic bomb may be made with highly enriched uranium or with plutonium. In 1981 Israeli aircraft attacked a new research reactor near Baghdad in Iraq which France had contracted to fuel with highly enriched uranium; the Israelis said they believed that Iraq was trying to acquire bomb material (although it had accepted IAEA inspection). Israel itself was widely believed to have produced material for bombs;

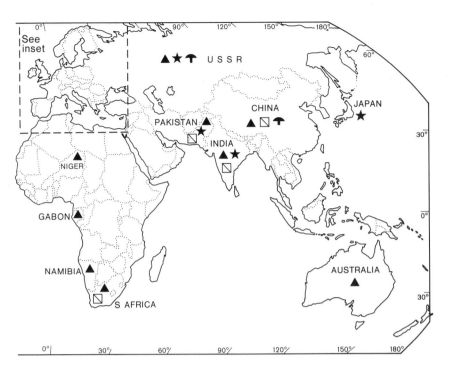

although it had no nuclear power plants, it had other reactors, which had not been submitted to inspection. All reactors produce plutonium; but, before a weapon can be made from it, it has to be separated out from the used reactor fuel by reprocessing. Few countries have the necessary reprocessing plants as yet, but these few include several 'near-nuclear' states.

5 Some key minerals

Coal, oil and uranium (*2, 3, 4*) are not the only mineral resources that can give a country special significance. There are a number of minerals which are not sources of energy but are concentrated in a few areas to a degree that can have important consequences, both economic and political.

For example, Malaysia, Indonesia, Thailand and Bolivia have in recent years produced more than half of the world's output of tin – a versatile substance, nowadays used for many other purposes as well as for canning. Australia, Guinea and Jamaica have produced more than half of the world's output of bauxite, the ore from which aluminium is made. (The making of aluminium requires huge supplies of electricity, and the smelters are sited near energy sources more often than near bauxite

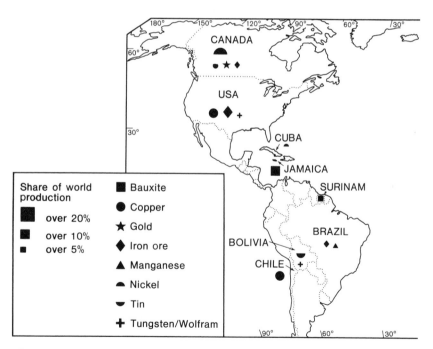

Share of world production

■ over 20%
■ over 10%
■ over 5%

■ Bauxite
● Copper
★ Gold
◆ Iron ore
▲ Manganese
⏝ Nickel
⏝ Tin
✦ Tungsten/Wolfram

mines; for this reason, Canada and Norway rank high among the producing and exporting countries.)

Among the ferro-alloys, which are used in the production of many kinds of steel, three-quarters of all nickel is mined in Canada, USSR, Australia and New Caledonia, nearly half of all tungsten (wolfram) in China and the USSR, and two-thirds of all manganese in the USSR, South Africa and Gabon. Not marked on the map are chrome (major producers: USSR, South Africa, Zimbabwe, Turkey, Philippines) and cobalt (Zaire, USA, Zambia, Canada, Morocco, Finland).

South Africa and the USSR are much the biggest sources of gold, and, together with Zaire, of diamonds. Both gold and diamonds have industrial uses; but the primary role that gold plays in the world economy is still that of serving as a form of monetary reserves – so, when international tension rises and confidence in national currencies is weakened, the price of gold is likely to rise, to the benefit of the exporting countries.

New developments can change a map such as this one quickly and

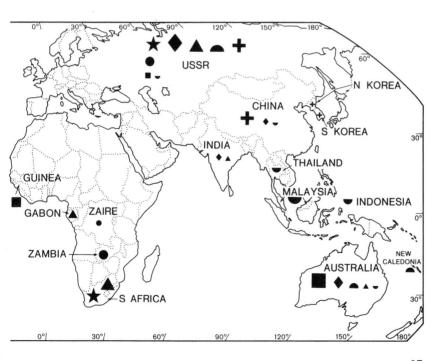

dramatically. Australia's appearance among the foremost mining states, for example, is a very recent event. If this map had been produced in the 1960s it would have shown no markings on that country.

Western Europe and Japan are not well endowed with the minerals marked on the map – although in recent years France and Greece together have accounted for 6% of all production of bauxite; Japan, the Scandinavian states and Spain, for 3% of copper; Britain, France, Norway, Spain and Sweden, for 7% of iron ore. In general, however, European and Japanese industries depend heavily on imported materials. And, while much processing of those materials has until now been done in western Europe and Japan, many mineral-exporting countries are now eager to do more of the processing themselves. Chile and Zambia each refine more copper nowadays than any European country does; tin is mostly smelted in the countries where it is mined; steel production has grown rapidly in Brazil, India, Venezuela and other third-world countries that produce iron ore.

Much mineral wealth lies beneath the sea. New technologies have recently opened up the prospect of valuable metals being 'mined' from the deep ocean floor, in areas which, even under the proposed new code of sea law (6), will be out beyond the limits of coastal states' jurisdiction. Exploration has shown that in many places the ocean floor is sprinkled with 'manganese nodules' – lumps containing nickel, copper and cobalt as well as manganese. The states that export these minerals (including Canada, Chile, Zaire and Zambia) have naturally been concerned, in the negotiations about an international regime for seabed mining, to get limitations imposed so that the market would not be 'flooded' by the potentially enormous haul from the depths.

6 Sea law

Seven-tenths of the earth's surface is covered by the 'seven seas'. Until the middle of this century, nearly all of this vast area was regarded as 'the high seas', under no national jurisdiction. Maritime nations upheld the principle of freedom of navigation. Most coastal states claimed territorial waters extending only 3 nautical miles from shore (100 nautical miles are about 115 land miles or 185 kilometres). But sea claims were getting bigger; 12-mile limits became more numerous, and some states even proclaimed 200-mile ones. United Nations conferences on the law of the sea (UNCLOS) in 1958 and 1960 failed to resolve the problems. In the 1950s and 1960s Britain, Iceland and Norway were among the states that became particularly embroiled over fishing rights. The 1958 conference did, however, produce a convention on rights to the oil and gas beneath the relatively shallow waters of 'continental shelf' areas such as the North Sea (22).

From 1974 to 1982 the third UNCLOS negotiated a whole new code of sea law suited to an age in which disputes over fisheries, offshore oil and freedom of navigation were becoming more numerous and dangerous. This code was approved in April 1982, but the lack of unanimity left much uncertainty about how long it might still take to bring the code into effect.

It was agreed to authorize 12-mile limits and to allow each coastal state, in addition, a 200-mile 'exclusive economic zone' (EEZ), in which it would control both mineral and fishing rights – as well as having mineral rights on the 'shelf' (which in some places extends far more than 200 miles from shore). During the 1970s claims to EEZs were announced by most of the coastal states, which thus 'jumped the gun' by asserting claims based on the new code without waiting for it to come into force.

A third of all the oceans are brought under the jurisdiction of the coastal states by the introduction of EEZs. These zones affect the whole of the Caribbean and Mediterranean as well as large parts of the oceans. Even a tiny island may be entitled to a sea zone of about 130,000 square miles. Between states that are close neighbours, the division of potentially overlapping EEZ and shelf zones can often be settled by drawing a median line, equidistant from their coasts; but many disputes have

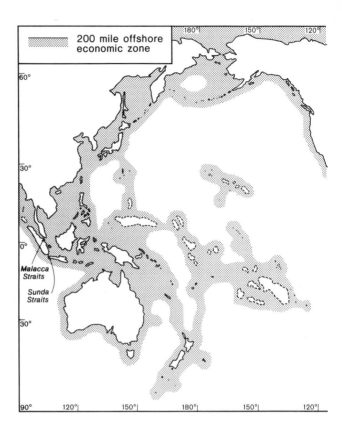

200 mile offshore economic zone

already arisen over this (e.g. between Greece and Turkey, Libya and Malta, Colombia and Venezuela, Norway and Russia – *22, 26, 38, 70*). Disputes about islands can also be intensified when claims to large sea areas go with them; this is relevant both to Argentina's quarrel with Chile over the Beagle Channel islets and to its seizing of the Falklands and South Georgia in 1982 (*72, 73*).

The new code will give coastal states more power to limit marine pollution (e.g. tankers dumping residual oil at sea), but it upholds the general right of free navigation in EEZs. It also upholds freedom of navigation through straits of international importance, even though the approval of 12-mile limits may mean that many of these straits become the territorial waters of the coastal states on each side; the Dover and Gibraltar straits, for example, are respectively only 21 and 9 miles wide at

20

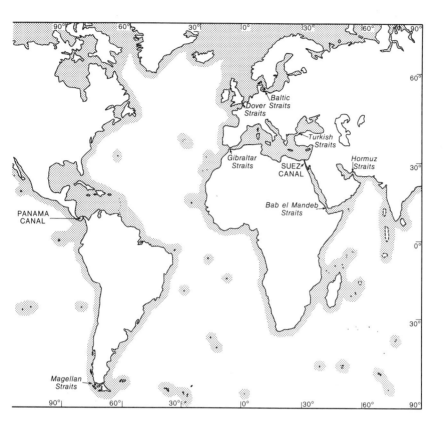

their narrowest points. These principles do not apply to the Suez and Panama canals, although they, too, are of great importance for world shipping; they have their own regimes, as do the Turkish straits (Dardanelles and Bosphorus), where the two coasts both belong to the same country.

The new code lays down the principle that the minerals on the deep ocean floor, out beyond the coastal states' EEZs and shelf zones, are 'the common heritage of mankind'. An international regime has been devised (5) to ensure that these minerals should not all go to the first-comers – the countries that are already developing the necessary technology. Disputes about this regime led several states, including the USA, to hold back from signing the convention embodying the new sea law code in December 1982.

7 Three worlds?

Between the late 1940s and the early 1960s the world's nations seemed to become divided into three groups – often labelled as 'east', 'west' and 'south'. The USSR and the east European states which it had brought under its control during and after the 1939–45 war (*13*, *16*) sealed themselves off behind their 'iron curtain', and the civil war in China added it, too, to the communist 'eastern block'. Fear of Soviet armed strength led most of the democratic European states to seek closer links with the USA and Canada (*20*); a few of them – Austria, Finland, Ireland, Sweden, Switzerland – remained 'neutral', but the basic 'east–west' division became very clear. The two camps possessed, between them, the greater part of the world's economic power (*2*) as well as of its modern armaments (*10*), and the conflicts and tensions arising from such

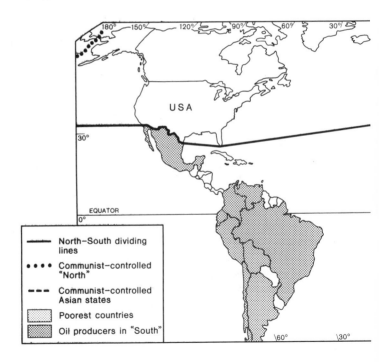

east–west issues as Berlin, Korea and Cuba (*18, 58, 70*) had global repercussions. But the 'third-world' states of Latin America, the Caribbean, Africa, southern Asia and the Pacific, a majority of which emerged from European colonial rule in this period, were in general much more concerned with 'north–south' issues than with east–west ones.

In 1961 the 'non-aligned' movement was founded at a 25-nation conference held at Belgrade but mainly representing Asian and African governments, with India and Egypt playing star roles. The movement's membership grew steadily as more 'new nations' became independent; after 20 years it included nearly 100 third-world governments. These governments pressed for completion of the decolonizing process; for more generous terms of trade and development aid from the relatively rich 'north'; and, in principle, for northern non-intervention in the south's affairs – although, in practice, third-world states often sought northern states' help in their local quarrels, and fought local wars with arms obtained from northern suppliers (sometimes, under agreements that compromised their non-alignment).

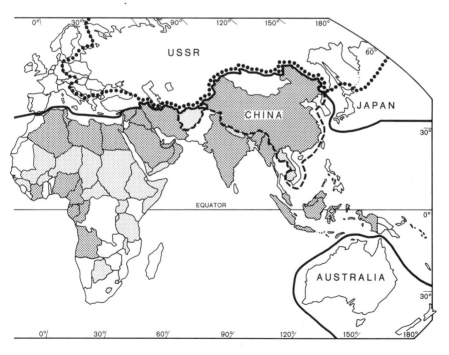

By 1982 the pattern of division had become more complex. Although more unity had been achieved in western Europe (*19*), the western alliance system was, for various reasons, under strain (*20, 26*). In the east, the USSR still controlled most of eastern Europe (but not Jugoslavia or Albania – *17*); it had occupied Afghanistan and acquired a sphere of influence in Indochina (*49, 60, 61*); but it had been quarrelling bitterly for two decades with China (*53*). China was competing with the Russians for influence in the third world, and in some situations it had even lined up with the west against them. Among the 'non-aligned' states, some were in practice inclined towards the west, some towards Russia or China. In the late 1970s the most pro-Soviet members (notably Cuba, Ethiopia and Vietnam) tried hard to pull the whole non-aligned movement closer to the USSR, which claimed to be its 'natural ally'. This campaign caused a new rift among the third-world states, which were already troubled by a number of quarrels in their ranks (*37, 39, 48, 59*).

In economic negotiations with the 'north', the third-world states could usually unite. But even here rifts among them appeared, particularly when the oil price increases in the 1970s hit the poorest countries very hard and opened up an obvious gap between those states that exported oil or were self-sufficient in it, and those that had to pay the new prices (*3*). The oil-exporting states made contributions to development aid funds, but the bulk of these funds was still provided by the west (and very little by the USSR).

East, west, north and south may be useful terms, but they are not accurate ones. Japan can be lumped in with the 'west', Australia and New Zealand with the 'north', disregarding geography in both cases; but is China 'east' or 'south'? The north is mainly 'white' and richer, the south mainly 'non-white' and poorer; in official jargon the two are often labelled 'developed' and 'developing'; but all these distinctions are blurred. The 'developing' south includes some states that are now richer than many of the northern ones, and others – among the poorest – that are hardly developing at all.

8 One world?

In the 1930s there were only 70 sovereign states. Now there are over 160, mainly because nearly all the former European dependencies in Africa, Asia, the Pacific and the Caribbean (9, 27, 65, 70) have become independent. World government is still a distant dream. But since 1945 a world organization, the United Nations, has provided its members with means of working together – when enough of them are willing – to avert conflicts or at least limit their consequences.

The UN's original membership was very lopsided. It excluded the countries defeated in the 1939–45 war; only a few Asian and African states were then independent; of the 51 founders, 20 were Latin American states; the USSR insisted on getting two extra seats, nominally for its Ukrainian and Byelorussian republics (14, 15), and thus obtained three votes, which it still uses. By 1982 the membership was 157 – more cumbrous, but more complete, and more balanced in proportion to the populations of the world's main regions. During the 1970s West Germany, East Germany, Vietnam and 20 newly independent ex-colonies had joined the UN, and China's seat, long held by the government that now ruled only in Taiwan (55), had been taken over by the government that ruled China. The only remaining non-members were Switzerland, South Korea, North Korea, and a few very small European and Pacific states such as Monaco and Tuvalu. The third-world states now have a large majority (whenever they close ranks) in the UN Assembly; but in the Security Council each of five major powers has a permanent seat and can veto decisions on conflicts and serious disputes, on Charter amendments and on the choice of a new chief for the UN Secretariat.

Under the UN flag, soldiers from many different countries have fought a war to resist aggression in Korea (58), and have manned small peacekeeping forces and military observer groups which have halted or mitigated conflicts in other troubled areas. With widely varying amounts of success, the UN has been involved in attempts to deal with disputes and conflicts in almost every part of the world. By 1982 it had seen 11 trust territories achieve independence or merge with neighbouring states. With its 'family' of agencies, it had channelled international aid to millions of refugees and to virtually all the countries of the 'third world'.

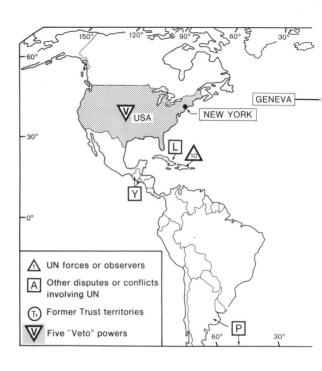

Operations by UN forces or military observer groups

1 Greek northern frontier, 1946–49 (*17*)
2 Indonesia, 1947–51 (*63*)
3 Palestine/Israel, Egypt, Lebanon, 1947– (*42–44*)
4 Kashmir, 1948– (*50*)
5 Korea, 1950–53 (*58*)
6 Congo/Zaire, 1960–64 (*32*)
7 West Irian, 1962–63 (*63*)
8 (North) Yemen, 1963–64 (*45*)
9 Cyprus, 1964– (*26*)
10 Dominican Republic, 1965 (*70*)
11 India–Pakistan frontier, 1965–66 (*51*)

Former UN Trust Territories

T1 Togolands (*36*)
T2 Camerouns (*36*)
T3 Rwanda, Burundi (*35*)
T4 Tanganyika (*35*)
T5 Somalia (*35*)
T6 NE New Guinea (*63*)
T7 Nauru (*65*)
T8 Western Samoa (*65*)

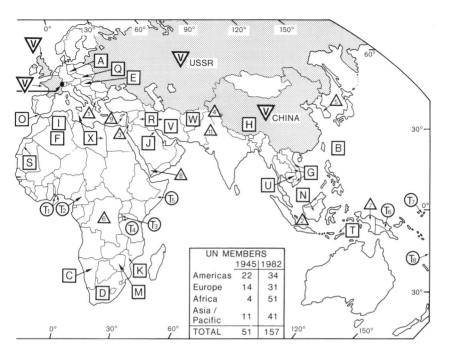

UN MEMBERS		
	1945	1982
Americas	22	34
Europe	14	31
Africa	4	51
Asia / Pacific	11	41
TOTAL	51	157

Other disputes and conflicts involving the UN

A West Berlin, 1948–49 (*18*)
B Taiwan, 1949–71 (*55*)
C Namibia, 1949– (*34*)
D South Africa, 1952– (*33*)
E Hungary, 1956 (*16*)
F Algeria, 1956–61 (*38*)
G Indochina, 1958–66 (*60*)
H Tibet, 1959–61 (*52*)
I Tunisia, 1961 (*38*)
J Kuwait, 1961–63 (*46*)
K Angola, Mozambique, etc., 1961–75 (*31*)
L Cuba, 1962 (*70*)

M Rhodesia/Zimbabwe, 1962–79 (*32*)
N Borneo, 1963–65 (*62*)
O Gibraltar, 1965– (*25*)
P Falklands, 1965– (*73*)
Q Czechoslovakia, 1968 (*16*)
R Iran–Iraq, 1974– (*48*)
S Western Sahara, 1974– (*39*)
T East Timor, 1975– (*63*)
U Cambodia, 1979– (*61*)
V Iran–USA, 1979–80 (*47*)
W Afghanistan–USSR, 1979– (*49*)
X Malta–Libya, 1980 (*38*)
Y Belize–Guatemala, 1981 (*70*)

9 Commonwealth

The Commonwealth is an association of states which were once parts of the British empire. The old Dominions were confirmed in their effective independence by the 1931 Statute of Westminster; India and Pakistan became independent in 1947; the 'decolonization' of the rest of the empire followed, and by 1962 there were 15 sovereign Commonwealth member states; by 1972, 32 of them; and by 1982, 47 – which virtually completed the process.

Membership requires a country's free choice, and its acceptance by the other states. When Burma became independent in 1948 and South Yemen in 1967, they chose not to become members. The former Irish Free State left the Commonwealth when it became a republic in 1949 (24). South Africa (33) left in 1961. Pakistan withdrew in 1972, when Bangladesh – formerly East Pakistan – was admitted (51). The question of membership did not arise for some states which, although they had been under British control for a time, had not been formally regarded as British dependencies. However, the British–French condominium of the New Hebrides became a Commonwealth member when it reached independence, as Vanuatu, in 1980 (65).

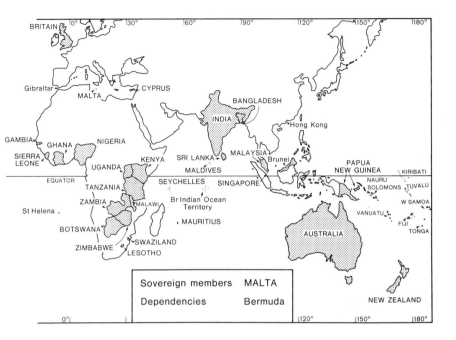

Four of the smallest Commonwealth states – Maldives, Nauru, St Vincent and Tuvalu – are 'special members'; they do not take part in the meetings of heads of government (prime ministers and presidents) that are held every 2 years, but they participate in other joint activities. Even states that have withdrawn have in some cases – notably, Ireland's – retained some advantages of membership. The Commonwealth governments have set up a joint Secretariat, a technical co-operation fund, and other institutions, whose services have been particularly valued by the smaller and poorer member states.

The member governments are often divided on international issues. But predictions that Britain's entry into the EEC (*19*) would mean the end of the Commonwealth proved unfounded. Precisely because it now serves as a bridge between nations with different viewpoints and interests, its members seem to feel that it has a unique value in a divided world.

The member states are listed here by regions, with dates of admission (except for the older members). The republics and the states that have their own monarchies are indicated. In each of the remaining countries

29

Queen Elizabeth II (whom all members also acknowledge as Head of the Commonwealth) is the head of State, represented – except in Britain – by a governor-general, whose appointment is a matter for that country alone; the title is the only vestige of the former imperial authority.

Africa		*Americas*		*Europe*	
r Botswana	1966	Antigua	1981	Britain	
r Gambia	1965	Bahamas	1973	r Cyprus	1961
r Ghana	1957	Barbados	1966	r Malta	1964
r Kenya	1963	Belize	1981		
o Lesotho	1966	Canada		*Pacific*	
r Malawi	1964	r Dominica	1978	Australia	
Mauritius	1968	r Grenada	1974	Fiji	1970
r Nigeria	1960	r Guyana	1966	r Kiribati	1979
r Seychelles	1976	Jamaica	1962	r Nauru	1968
r Sierra Leone	1961	St Lucia	1979	New Zealand	
o Swaziland	1968	St Vincent	1979	Papua New Guinea	1975
r Tanzania	1961	r Trinidad	1962	Solomons	1978
r Uganda	1962			o Tonga	1970
r Zambia	1964	*Asia*		r Tuvalu	1978
r Zimbabwe	1980	r Bangladesh	1972	r Vanuatu	1980
		r India	1947	r Western Samoa	1962
		o Malaysia	1957		
		r Maldives	1982		
		r Singapore	1965		
		r Sri Lanka	1948		

(o=own monarchy, r=republic)

10 The long arm of war

In 1945 the American atomic bombs dropped on Hiroshima and Nagasaki brought the Japanese war to a swift end, and may well have saved far more lives than they took. But, ever since then, the destructive power of nuclear weapons has caused widespread horror and fear; and the great increase in that power has even aroused fears that a full-scale nuclear war might destroy mankind. The world entered the 1980s without any more nuclear weapons being used in war, but its affairs have been strongly influenced by their mere existence; by their being brandished as a threat of force, or as a deterrent to the use of force; by some states' attempts to acquire them, and by others' efforts to curb their proliferation.

In 1964, when China staged its first bomb test, it joined the USA, USSR, Britain and France as the fifth nuclear-armed power. In 1974

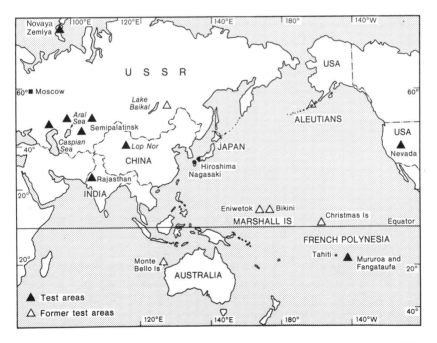

India set off an underground nuclear blast, but claimed that its purpose was non-military. No other countries were known to have staged nuclear explosions up to 1982; but several were suspected to be close to acquiring 'the bomb' (4).

In the 1963 'partial test ban' treaty the USA, USSR and Britain promised that future tests would be staged only in underground cavities – so that they would not send masses of radioactive debris into the atmosphere. France followed suit in 1974; China went on with above-ground explosions.

Nuclear strategy was transformed after 1957, when first the Russians and then the Americans developed and deployed intercontinental ballistic missiles (ICBMs) with ranges of well over 5000 miles. In 1982, each superpower's ICBMs were capable of delivering several thousand warheads on to the other's territory. Each was keeping at sea a number of submarines that could hit the other power with nuclear missiles; each also had long-range aircraft capable of carrying nuclear weapons. Britain and France had acquired smaller numbers of missile-firing submarines; France had also deployed land-based missiles whose range extended to Moscow; China had acquired ICBMs.

As well as general anxiety about the possibility of a nuclear war, there were more specific fears about the pressures that a nuclear-armed power could apply if it did not face an adequate deterrent. In the west, one fear that took shape in the early 1980s was that the USSR, whose newest ICBMs were very accurate and powerful, might use them to destroy nearly all the American ICBMs in a 'first strike'. The American submarines could retaliate by destroying Russian cities, but could not prevent a second wave of Soviet missiles destroying American cities – so Russia might calculate that the Americans would give in rather than choose mutual devastation. With possibilities like these in mind, the USSR might feel free to seek gains in various parts of the world without much risk of being challenged by the USA.

In Europe, another fear had emerged: that Russia, which was deploying hundreds of new medium-range missiles (up to 3000 miles range) aimed at western Europe, could put pressure on European states by threatening to attack them while warning the USA not to intervene. To allay this fear, the NATO governments (20) adopted in 1979 a plan to deploy new American medium-range and 'cruise' missiles in Europe by 1983 if Russia would not remove or reduce its array of missiles aimed at western Europe. But the NATO plan also aroused European opposition; and the Russians hinted that, if it was carried out, they might deploy

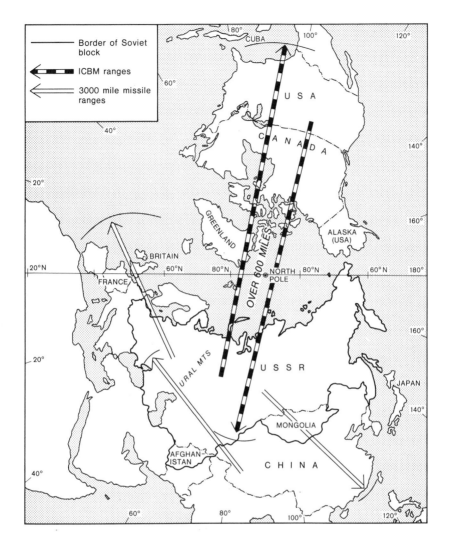

more medium-range missiles, this time aimed at the USA – presumably from Cuba. In 1962 the Russians had tried to place nuclear missiles capable of hitting the USA in Cuba (70); but their preparations were detected and, after a period of great tension, they were obliged to abandon that attempt.

11 Arctic

The first man ever to reach the North Pole was Robert Peary, who got there in 1909, using dog-drawn sledges. By 1958 other Americans were able to pass under the Pole in a nuclear-powered submarine which travelled beneath the ice from Pacific to Atlantic. By then, too, Scandinavian airliners were crossing the Arctic on regular flights between Europe and Japan by way of Alaska. Things have moved fast in the far north. Russia has staged nuclear-bomb tests in Novaya Zemlya (*10*), including, in 1961, the biggest man-made explosion yet recorded. There are coalmines in Svalbard (Spitsbergen – *22*); huge new oilfields near Prudhoe Bay on the North Slope in Alaska (*67*); and oil and gas have also been found on and around Canada's Arctic islands (*68*).

Political change has come to the region. Alaska became the 49th state of the USA in 1959. Iceland's constitutional links with Denmark were ended when it became an independent republic in 1944. Greenland, a former Danish dependency given county status in 1953, obtained 'home rule' in 1979 (*21*).

In the 1970s the Alaska oilfields provided a major new source of non-OPEC oil (*3*). In the early 1980s there was controversy over the plans to pipe more Soviet gas to western Europe from fields near the Ob river estuary in north-western Siberia. In the Soviet sector of the Arctic, development had long been linked with the large-scale use of prisoners as a labour force, from the coalmines around Vorkuta to the goldmines of the Kolyma region. Whole districts, especially in north-eastern Siberia, were run by the KGB as gigantic 'gulags' (*15*).

During the short Arctic summers, ships equipped for icebreaking can reach ports along the whole Siberian coast. But the only ice-free part of the Soviet Arctic coast is the stretch around Murmansk near the Norwegian border. Only from the naval bases in this sector can Russia's warships, and its missile-firing nuclear submarines, move into the Atlantic without passing through straits in the Baltic or the Mediterranean.

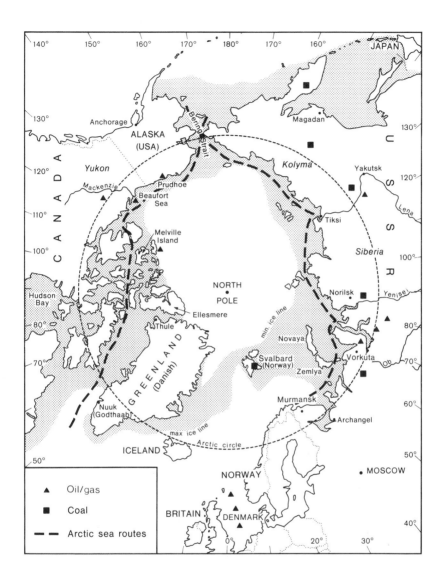

140° 150° 160° 170° 180° 170° 160° JAPAN

130° Anchorage Magadan 130°

ALASKA
(USA)

Yukon Kolyma Yakutsk

120° 120°

Mackenzie Prudhoe Tiksi

110° Beaufort
Sea 110°

Melville
Island Siberia 100°

C A N A D A 100°

NORTH
POLE Norilsk

Hudson
Bay Ellesmere 80°

80° Thule Novaya

GREENLAND Svalbard Vorkuta 70°
70° (Danish) (Norway) Zemlya

Nuuk Murmansk 60°
(Godthaab)

max ice line Archangel
Arctic circle

ICELAND 50°

50°

NORWAY MOSCOW

▲ Oil/gas

■ Coal BRITAIN DENMARK 40°

▬ ▬ Arctic sea routes 0° 20° 30°

35

12 Antarctic

Scientific bases in Antarctica have been maintained by several nations since the 1950s. Claims to sovereignty over sectors of the frozen continent's $5\frac{1}{2}$ million square miles have been made by Australia, Britain, France, New Zealand and Norway, which recognize each other's claims; and by Argentina and Chile, whose claims overlap with Britain's and with each other's.

In 1959 these seven nations, together with Belgium, Japan, South Africa, the USA and USSR, signed the Antarctic Treaty. Other nations later acceded to the treaty; of these, West Germany and Poland had by 1982 mounted enough research activity to qualify for full voting rights alongside the original 12 members. (Brazil, China and India were also showing their interest.) The treaty barred new claims, 'froze' the existing ones and did not commit signatories to recognizing any. It declared that Antarctica should be used only for peaceful purposes, and that each signatory could send observers to any part of it to see that the treaty was not being violated.

The treaty applied to the area south of latitude 60° South. In 1980 the treaty states signed a convention on conservation of marine living resources which applied to the much larger area encircled by the Antarctic Convergence – the line where warmer water overlays the near-freezing Antarctic surface water. The living resources in these waters include huge amounts of shrimp-like krill, which the Japanese and Russians have been particularly active in harvesting.

The British Antarctic Territory covers the mainland sector between longitudes 20° and 80° West and those adjacent islands that lie south of 60° South. Like the rest of Antarctica, it has no permanent population. Until 1962 it had been part of the Falkland Islands and Dependencies (which also include South Georgia and the South Sandwich Islands). After 1962, its administration – which, as sealing and whaling activity had ended, mainly concerned the scientific bases – was still handled through the Falklands (73).

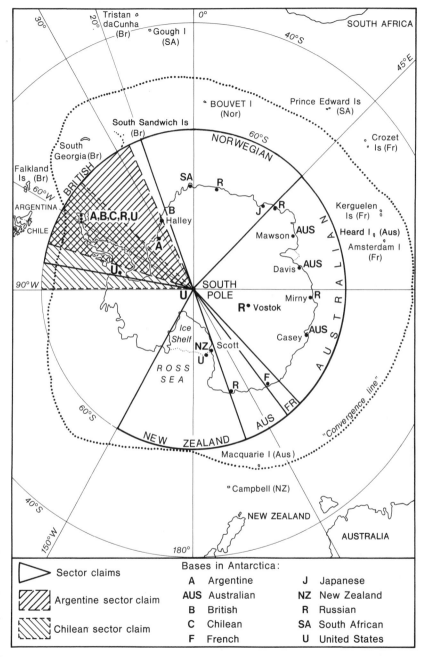

Tristan daCunha (Br)
°Gough I (SA)
0°
SOUTH AFRICA
40°S
45°E
30°
20°
BOUVET I (Nor)
Prince Edward Is (SA)
60°S
NORWEGIAN
Crozet Is (Fr)
South Sandwich Is (Br)
South Georgia(Br)
BRITISH
Falkland Is (Br)
60°W
ARGENTINA
A,B,C,R,U
SA
R
J
R
Mawson
AUS
Kerguelen Is (Fr)
Heard I (Aus)
Amsterdam I (Fr)
CHILE
Halley
B
A
Davis
AUS
U.
90°W
U
SOUTH POLE
Mirny
R
R• Vostok
AUSTRALIA
Ice Shelf
Casey
AUS
NZ Scott
U•
ROSS SEA
F
R
FR
AUS
60°S
NEW ZEALAND
"Convergence line"
Macquarie I (Aus)
40°S
°Campbell (NZ)
150°W
180°
NEW ZEALAND
AUSTRALIA

Sector claims

Argentine sector claim

Chilean sector claim

Bases in Antarctica:

A   Argentine   J   Japanese
AUS Australian   NZ   New Zealand
B   British   R   Russian
C   Chilean   SA   South African
F   French   U   United States

13 Divided Europe

When Nazi Germany's hold on Europe was broken in 1944–45 (*18*), the advancing Russian army imposed Soviet control on Poland, Hungary, Rumania and Bulgaria, and on parts of Germany and (until 1955) Austria. Communist regimes, then closely linked with Russia, were also established in Jugoslavia and Albania. An 'iron curtain of silence' (in Winston Churchill's words) fell across the middle of Europe, and the peoples east of it were deprived of free contact (*16*). Two gaps in the 'curtain' remained: West Berlin, surrounded by Soviet-held territory but garrisoned by American, British and French troops (*18*); and Czechoslovakia, where communist rule was not imposed so quickly as in other east European countries. But in 1948 a Soviet-backed communist coup turned Czechoslovakia into one more police state, and Russia also blockaded West Berlin in an attempt to break its fragile links with the west. In the same year, Jugoslavia's communist rulers broke free from the Soviet block (*17*).

Russia made formal alliances with its east European 'satellite' states, whose armed forces were in practice already under Soviet control; in 1955 these alliances were consolidated as the Warsaw Pact. Russia's economic grip on its satellites was formalized by the creation in 1949 of the Council for Mutual Economic Aid (CMEA – more often called Comecon). East Germany is included in both the Warsaw Pact and Comecon. Albania withdrew from both when it quarrelled with Russia in the 1960s. Jugoslavia kept out of the Pact, but became an associate of Comecon in 1964. The Warsaw Pact's true nature was revealed when Russia forced East Germany, Poland, Hungary and even Bulgaria to join it in invading their 'ally' Czechoslovakia in 1968. Rumania did not join in that invasion; its communist rulers have not always toed the Soviet line.

In 1975, at the 35-nation Conference on Security and Co-operation in Europe (CSCE), all the European governments, except Albania's, signed the Helsinki Agreement. This included promises that they would all promote freedom of contact and movement between their countries, including the USSR. But the Soviet block's regimes failed to keep their Helsinki promises. They ignored the appeals made to them at subsequent CSCE review conferences held at Belgrade in 1977–78 and at Madrid in

1980–83, and they persecuted the small 'Helsinki groups' formed in the communist countries, which tried to ask their rulers to keep their promises. So the iron curtain across Europe remained in place, preventing Europeans from achieving the security and co-operation that were the CSCE's proclaimed goals.

14 Russia's territorial gains

The USSR gained nearly 200,000 square miles of territory in Europe during and after the 1939–45 war – mostly taken from its allies or from states with which it had made non-aggression pacts. Its gains gave it a long Baltic coastline and brought it to the Danube mouth.

In 1939 it occupied eastern Poland and invaded Finland, forcing the Finns to cede part of Karelia. In 1940 it annexed Estonia, Latvia and Lithuania (which, like Finland, had freed themselves from Russia's rule after its 1917 revolutions) and forced Rumania to cede Bessarabia and northern Bukovina. After the war it retained all these gains, and also took Transcarpathia (Ruthenia) from Czechoslovakia; more territory from Finland, including Petsamo, the Finns' only Arctic port; and northern East Prussia, including Kaliningrad (formerly Königsberg), from Germany. Poland, alone among the victims, was 'compensated' for its losses in the east by being given areas taken from Germany in the west (*18*). The USSR's expansion brought it about 25 million more people, but two of the annexed areas were virtually depopulated: the Germans of East Prussia were deported, and the Finns in the ceded territory left their farms and homes and moved westward to avoid coming under Soviet rule.

The three former Baltic states became the Estonian, Latvian and Lithuanian republics of the USSR; part of Bessarabia became its Moldavian republic; the rest of the territory taken from Poland, Czechoslovakia and Rumania was incorporated in the Ukrainian and Byelorussian republics; the Kaliningrad region and the lands taken from Finland became parts of the USSR's Russian republic (*15*), and were mainly repopulated with Russians.

In the Far East, Russia took southern Sakhalin and the Kurile islands from Japan in 1945. It also reoccupied in 1945 the naval base of Port Arthur (Lushun) which tsarist Russia had held in 1898–1905; this was returned to China in 1955 (*53, 57*).

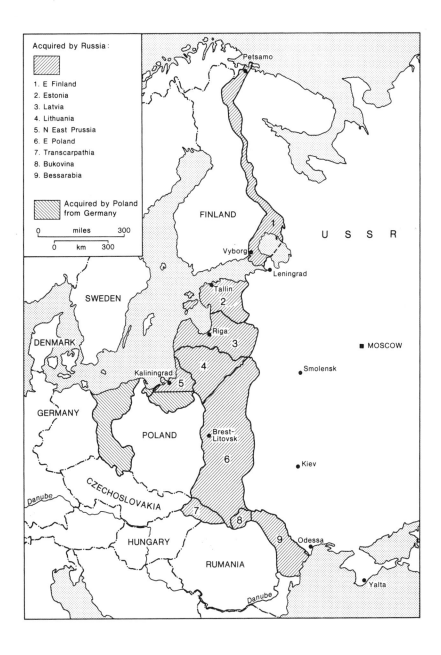

Acquired by Russia:

1. E Finland
2. Estonia
3. Latvia
4. Lithuania
5. N East Prussia
6. E Poland
7. Transcarpathia
8. Bukovina
9. Bessarabia

Acquired by Poland from Germany

0   miles   300
0   km   300

FINLAND

SWEDEN

DENMARK

GERMANY

POLAND

CZECHOSLOVAKIA

Danube

HUNGARY

RUMANIA

Danube

U S S R

Petsamo

Vyborg

Leningrad

Tallin

Riga

Kaliningrad

Brest-Litovsk

MOSCOW

Smolensk

Kiev

Odessa

Yalta

15 Russia (USSR)

Officially the Union of Soviet Socialist Republics (USSR, or Soviet Union), it is often called Russia, for brevity. In theory it is a federation of 15 republics – the Russian one (RSFSR) being the biggest and itself containing 16 smaller 'autonomous republics' for smaller nationalities (e.g. Bashkir, Buryat Mongolian, Kalmyk, Tartar, Tuva, Yakut). In

practice the USSR is even more tightly controlled from the centre than was its pre-1917 predecessor, the tsarist Russian empire.

Taking the Ural mountain range as the traditional dividing line, three-quarters of the country's territory is in Asia; but two-thirds of its population is in Europe, the greater part of Siberia being thinly peopled or empty. Russians now make up half of the total population, Ukrainians and Byelorussians another fifth, non-Slav peoples the remainder. Among the Central Asian peoples (Uzbeks, Kazakhs, etc.) population growth has become fast enough to cause concern in the ruling circles in Moscow, where it is feared that these peoples may eventually seek to get rid of Russian domination. Stirrings of national feeling have also persisted, in

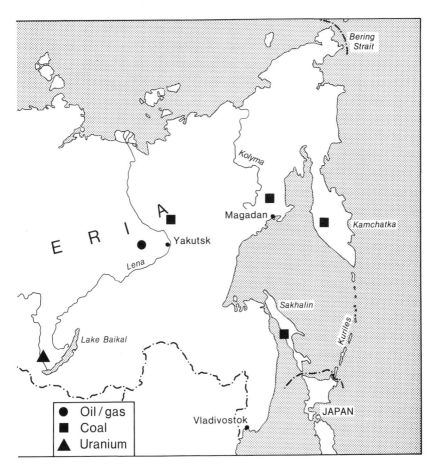

spite of repression, in the Baltic republics, the Caucasian ones (Armenia, Georgia, Azerbaijan) and the Ukraine (*14, 47, 49, 53*).

Both Russians and other nationalities have long been kept under tight control, however, by the elaborate and costly system of political policing which has set a special mark on the USSR in the form of the 'Gulag Archipelago' – the network of prison camp complexes all over the country. During Stalin's reign the 'gulag' population (for which no official figures are ever published) reached a record size, estimated at well over 10 million; it is now smaller, but still enormous. More than 2000 camp areas have been identified. Those that have acquired special notoriety include the ones around Vorkuta and Norilsk in the Arctic and Karaganda in Kazakhstan, and in the Far East the whole Kolyma region stretching north from Magadan.

Although the camps have taken several million lives, their surviving inmates have provided much of the labour force used to exploit the resources of Siberia and Central Asia. Those resources have enabled the USSR to become the world's biggest producer of oil, the second biggest producer of gold, and a major producer of coal and many other minerals (*2, 5*). Oil and gold have been particularly prominent among its exports.

Russia has recently also exported (by pipeline) natural gas, mainly from areas near or east of the Urals, to countries in both eastern and western Europe. In 1982 it was building a big new pipeline system to carry gas from north-western Siberia to western Europe, by way of Czechoslovakia (the shorter route across Poland being apparently ruled out for strategic reasons). The new pipeline was meant to export enough gas to the west to cover virtually the whole cost of the large imports of wheat and other food that Russia – a major exporter of grain before 1917 – had come to need after years of mismanagement of its 'collective farming'.

16 Eastern Europe

Russia, which had moved the whole of its own frontier westward during the 1939–45 war (*14*), then proceeded to impose Soviet-backed communist regimes on the countries along its border. This was a massive violation of the agreement concluded between the USSR, USA and Britain at Yalta, in the Crimea, in February 1945, 3 months before the final defeat of Nazi Germany. The Yalta agreement provided that all the liberated peoples of Europe must be enabled to 'create democratic institutions of their own choice'. For Poland, in particular, it required 'the holding of free and unfettered elections on the basis of universal suffrage and secret ballot'. Russia, however, ignored these pledges in the countries that its army had occupied. It imprisoned their leading non-communists (including leaders of the Polish resistance, who were lured to Moscow by promise of safe-conduct), and staged fraudulent elections which installed communist-led governments. The only exception was Czechoslovakia, where the communists were, for a time, content with a share in a coalition government; but they got a hold on the police and army, and in 1948 they seized power in a Soviet-backed coup and imposed on Czechoslovakia a regime similar to those in other east European countries. (Rather ironically, these regimes were then usually called 'people's democracies'.) Freedom of speech, association, and movement were abolished, and no free elections were ever held.

In 1955 Austria, where democracy had been restored in 1945, accepted a treaty that committed it to permanent neutrality, and Russia withdrew its troops from the zone in the north and east of Austria which they had been occupying. The Soviet government gave the 'Austrian model' a lot of publicity, with the aim of neutralizing West Germany; but stirrings in eastern Europe ensued. In 1956, after a brief revolt at Poznan, Russia granted the Poles a limited degree of autonomy. This encouraged the Hungarians to defy their masters. A coalition government was formed in Budapest and proposed that Hungary should withdraw from the Warsaw Pact (*13*). A large Russian army was sent in, which crushed the Hungarian revolution; but 200,000 Hungarians escaped to the west during the conflict.

In Czechoslovakia, mounting resentment of the regime's brutality brought a change in the communist leadership in 1968. The new leaders began to try to make reforms that would give the system 'a human face', but they assured Russia that they would remain loyal to the Warsaw Pact. The Soviet government, however, first tried to cow them into abandoning their reform programme by staging manoeuvres and troop movements, and, when this failed, it launched a full-scale invasion. Soviet forces entered Czechoslovakia from north, east and south, bringing with them as unenthusiastic 'allies' contingents of troops from East Germany, Poland, Hungary and Bulgaria. Repression succeeded reform, another puppet government was installed, and Soviet troops were stationed in Czechoslovakia, which had not previously had a permanent Russian garrison.

In Poland the 1970s saw outbreaks of mass protest (particularly in 1970 and 1976), provoked by the regime's economic mismanagement as well as by its repressive nature; these were violently suppressed. In 1980 there was an unprecedentedly widespread wave of strikes – which are illegal in communist states – and the regime was obliged to negotiate with the striking workers and to permit the forming of a free trade union organization called Solidarnosc (Solidarity). Farmers were later able to form a similar organization. For more than a year the negotiating went on and some compromises were achieved; the Russian forces in Poland did not intervene, but the regime warned the unions that there might be a Soviet intervention if they went on demanding democratic reforms. In December 1981 the Polish army (which, like all Warsaw Pact forces, was ultimately under Soviet control) seized power, imposed martial law, arrested the union leaders and suppressed protest strikes by taking over industrial centres and enforcing the resumption of work under military discipline. Initial resistance to this coup was eventually broken in all Poland's cities, including Warsaw, Radom, Cracow, Poznan, Wroclaw (formerly Breslau), Katowice and other Silesian coalmining centres, and the shipbuilding ports of Szczecin (Stettin), Gdynia, and Gdansk (Danzig) – where Solidarity had won its first foothold in 1980.

The East German and Bulgarian regimes followed the Soviet line dutifully throughout all these events; the Rumanian one did not always do so, although it suppressed internal dissent as strictly as any of the other east European regimes (*17*, *18*).

SWEDEN

Gdynia
Gdansk
● Kaliningrad

EAST
Szczecin
POLAND
Berlin
Poznan
GERMANY
■ Warsaw
Wroclaw
● Radom
● Lublin
Prague
Katowice
CZECHO-
● Cracow
SLOVAKIA
Vienna ■
AUSTRIA
■ Budapest
HUNGARY
RUMANIA
Belgrade ■
■ Bucharest
JUGOSLAVIA
BULGARIA
Russian zone
1945–1955
● Sofia
ALBANIA

UNION
OF
SOVIET
SOCIALIST
REPUBLICS

0   miles   200
0   km   200

47

17 Jugoslavia and neighbours

After the 1939–45 war, communist regimes took power in Jugoslavia and Albania. They were not occupied by Russian troops, but for a time they both followed the Soviet line. Jugoslavia had a quarrel of its own with the western powers, over Trieste. In the 1947 Italian peace treaty Jugoslavia gained areas north and south of Trieste, but not the city itself, whose population was mainly Italian. A British and American garrison held Trieste until 1954, when Jugoslavia at last agreed that the city should go to Italy.

In 1948 Jugoslavia's communist rulers refused to go on taking orders from Moscow. This rift disrupted the joint Albanian–Jugoslav–Bulgarian support of communist rebels in Greece, and in 1949 the last of those rebel forces withdrew into Bulgaria. With western help, Jugoslavia withstood several years of threats and pressure from the Soviet block. It cultivated links with third-world countries, and in 1961 the 'non-aligned' movement was founded at a conference in Belgrade (7).

In the 1960s Albania's rulers sided with China in its quarrel with Russia, but in 1977 they broke with China and from then on their isolated, mountainous little country (population $2\frac{3}{4}$ million) claimed to be the only true communist state, accusing all the others of having betrayed the doctrines of Stalin.

The $1\frac{3}{4}$ million Albanians in Jugoslavia have presented a special problem. Multinational Jugoslavia is a federation of six republics. One of these, Serbia, includes two 'autonomous regions': in the north, Voivodina, whose population is partly Hungarian; in the south, Kosovo, which is mainly Albanian. Violent conflicts broke out in Kosovo in 1968 and again, on a larger scale, in 1981; unrest continued there in 1982. Some rioters in Pristina called for union with Albania, but the demand most often voiced was for Kosovo to be given the status of a republic within Jugoslavia. Signs of tension between Serbs and Croats also appeared at times; and, when Bulgaria wanted to pick a quarrel with Jugoslavia, it revived old claims on the Jugoslav part of Macedonia.

Bulgaria, whose Slav language resembles Russian, and which histori-cally looked to Russia for protection against Turkey, proved a loyal Soviet 'satellite'. Non-Slav Rumania, although a Warsaw Pact member,

repeatedly strayed from the Soviet line in foreign policy. It criticized Russia's invasion of Czechoslovakia, and it flirted with China and Jugoslavia. Its communist regime has, however, been as repressive as any in the Soviet block. After the crushing of the 1956 revolution in Hungary, Rumania took the opportunity to clamp down on its own Hungarian minority, abolishing the 'autonomous territory' in Transylvania, where most of them lived, and deporting thousands of them to the swamplands of the Dobruja.

18 Divided Germany

The Nazi regime that held power in Germany from 1933 to 1945 led it into a series of annexations and wars of conquest which, in the end, left it as a smaller country – and a divided one.

In 1938 Nazi Germany occupied Austria and (after the conference at Munich) forced the cession of the Sudetenland border regions of western Czechoslovakia (running all along its frontier with Germany). In 1939 it took over the rest of Czechoslovakia; demanded Danzig (now Gdansk), which was then a 'free city', serving Poland as a port; and, using Danzig as a pretext, invaded Poland – after making a pact with Russia under which the two powers then divided Poland between them. Britain and France, which had given guarantees to Poland, declared war on Germany. During the subsequent 6 years of war Germany, with its allies, at one stage controlled most of Europe, including a large part of Russia.

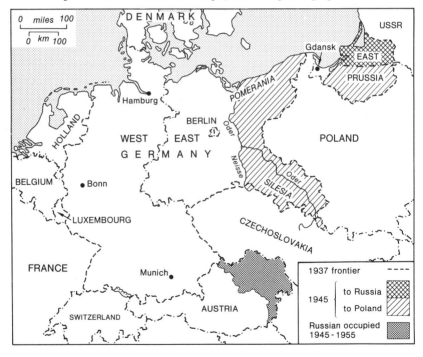

But by 1945 the Nazi empire was destroyed, and the advancing allied western and Soviet armies met in the middle of Germany.

Austria was re-established as a democratic republic, although the four allied powers kept troops there until 1955 (*16*). The Sudetenland was returned to Czechoslovakia and its German inhabitants were expelled. France took over the Saar – but returned it to Germany in 1957. Russia annexed northern East Prussia for itself and, expelling the inhabitants of

Silesia and the other parts of Germany east of the line of the Oder and Neisse rivers, assigned these areas to Poland (*14*).

The Germany that remained was divided in 1945 into four zones under the military administration of the USSR, USA, Britain and France. Berlin, which lay inside the Russian zone, was also divided into sectors garrisoned by the four powers. The Russians imposed in their zone a communist system similar to those they imposed in eastern Europe (*16*) and blocked western attempts to rebuild a democratic system for the whole of Germany. By 1948 the western allies had to give up hope of Soviet co-operation and put through reforms in their three zones alone. The Russians then blockaded West Berlin for a year; but a huge airlift mounted by the western allies kept its two million people fed. (In later years Russia often interfered with Berlin's communications with the west at times when it wanted to increase tension and to show its power to put a squeeze on the outpost city.)

Hopes of early German reunification had by now dwindled. The three western zones were united in 1949 to form the Federal Republic of Germany (FRG, usually called West Germany, population now 62 million), with its capital at Bonn. Russia established in its zone a communist state, the German Democratic Republic (GDR, or East Germany, population 17 million). In the 1950s several million people managed to escape from East Germany to the west, many of them by way of Berlin. The communist regime stopped this massive outflow by building in 1961 a heavily guarded 30-mile-long wall between the two halves of Berlin, and creating an equally formidable 'death strip' along the whole border between West and East Germany.

Large Soviet forces remained in East Germany, which became a member of the Soviet block's military Warsaw Pact. West Germany joined NATO (*20*), and the allied forces stationed there relinquished their postwar occupation status, but that status remained the basis for the presence of the American, British and French garrisons in West Berlin, and West Berlin was given a special relationship to the FRG without fully belonging to it.

Between 1970 and 1973 West Germany made treaties with the USSR, East Germany and Poland (which, among other things, confirmed the Oder–Neisse frontier line); and in 1972 the USSR, USA, Britain and France signed a new agreement on Berlin. But the country remained painfully divided, and although the Soviet and East German governments signed the 1975 Helsinki agreement (*13*), they still refused to let the people of the GDR have free contact with their fellow Germans in the west.

52

19 West European unities

In 1947 most of the non-communist European countries joined the Organization for European Economic Co-operation (OEEC), which was formed to handle the European Recovery Programme (or Marshall Plan) that massive American aid made possible. The OEEC was succeeded in 1961 by the OECD (Organization for Economic Co-operation and Development), whose 24 members included, outside Europe, Australia, Canada, Japan, New Zealand and the USA. OECD headquarters are in Paris.

From 1949 on, most of the European democracies sent ministers and members of parliament to the Council of Europe at Strasbourg, a mainly consultative body. It negotiated a number of conventions, including one on human rights, to adjudicate on which the European Court of Human Rights was established in 1959.

Western European Union (WEU), a seven-nation group, based in London, originated with the signing of the Brussels Treaty in 1948 by Britain, France, Belgium, Holland (the Netherlands) and Luxembourg. (The last three of these five countries had already formed a customs union, Benelux, which later became a fuller economic union.) Italy and West Germany joined WEU in 1955. The 1948 treaty reflected a disarmed postwar western Europe's fear of the large army that Russia was still keeping in Germany, and of Soviet intentions as revealed by the 1948 coup in Czechoslovakia (*13, 16*). WEU's economic and defence functions were eventually absorbed into the work of the EEC (see below) and NATO (*20*), but its consultative meetings continued.

The European Economic Community (EEC), often called the Common Market, was based on the 1957 Treaty of Rome, signed by six of the seven WEU countries – the missing one being Britain. Trade between the Six was made duty-free by stages; the last tariffs were abolished in 1968. The same six states had also created a European Coal and Steel Community (ECSC) and a European Atomic Energy Community (Euratom). They agreed to merge their three communities gradually into a single one, and in 1967 the three executive bodies were merged into a single European Commission, based in Brussels. The Six adopted a common agricultural policy (CAP), which involved an elaborate system of farm subsidies; removed barriers to the free movement of labour between their countries; and promoted integration in other ways, including the establishment of a European Parliament, whose budgetary and other powers were gradually increased – although the Council of Ministers retained ultimate authority in most respects.

Britain and other countries which did not want to take integration as far as the Six proposed, but did want to extend free trade in Europe, formed in 1960 the European Free Trade Association (EFTA), whose members had abolished tariffs on (non-farm) trade between them by 1967. EFTA placed its headquarters in Geneva.

In 1973 Britain and Denmark left EFTA and joined the EEC, and Ireland also joined the EEC. Greece became the Community's tenth member in 1981. All the seven remaining members of EFTA – Austria, Finland (an associate member), Iceland, Norway, Portugal, Sweden and Switzerland – signed free trade agreements with the EEC in 1972–73. As a result, almost complete free trade in industrial goods was achieved between all members of the two groupings by 1977.

A convention signed at Yaoundé, in Cameroun, in 1963 provided for development aid and access to EEC markets for 18 associated African states. These arrangements were enlarged, and extended to 28 other African, Caribbean and Pacific (ACP) states, by the convention signed at Lomé, in Togo, in 1975. By 1982, a total of 58 ACP states were thus linked to the EEC.

Although the Community has promoted free trade within Europe, and created a European grouping which is reasonably comparable in economic power to the USA and USSR (2), its members' efforts to develop a common foreign policy have had only limited success. Its protection and subsidizing of inefficient farming, with the consequent creation of large surpluses, some of which have been in effect 'dumped' outside the Community, have harmed more efficient food producers in other countries, including New Zealand (64); and its members have long been at odds over the adapting of their fisheries policy to the new situation created by the claiming of 200-mile-wide 'exclusive economic zones' of sea (6, 22). Fishery disputes were largely responsible for the decision not to join the Community taken by the Faroe islands, which are self-governing under the Danish crown, and for the vote to withdraw from the EEC that the people of Greenland recorded in a referendum after they had achieved similar autonomy in 1979 (21, 22).

ICELAND

Faroes

BRITAIN

IRELAND

DENMARK

NORWAY

SWEDEN

FINLAND

Belgium.................B
Netherlands............N
Luxembourg.............L

EEC: founder members

EEC: joined later

EFTA...................

N

B

L

WEST
GERMANY

FRANCE

SWITZ.

AUSTRIA

ITALY

PORTUGAL

SPAIN

TURKEY

0   miles   500

0   km   500

GREECE

55

20 Atlantic alliance

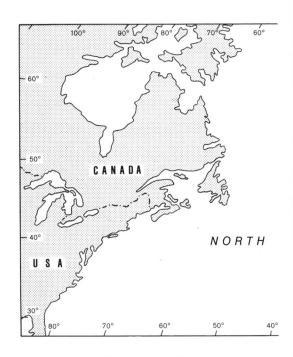

The five signatories of the 1948 Brussels Treaty (*19*), Britain, France, Belgium, Holland and Luxembourg, knowing that their united strength was not enough to provide a counter-balance to the military power that Russia was maintaining in central Europe, sought American support. Traditional American dislike of 'entangling alliances' was overcome after several menacing Soviet moves – the coup in Czechoslovakia, threats to Norway and Finland, the blockade of West Berlin (*13, 16, 18, 21*). In 1949 the United States and Canada joined with the Brussels Treaty five and with Denmark, Iceland, Italy, Norway and Portugal in signing the North Atlantic Treaty. The 12 allies pledged joint resistance to any attack on one of them.

In 1950 the invasion of South Korea (*58*) increased the allies' fears and led them to set up a command structure and to begin to create the more comprehensive North Atlantic Treaty Organization (NATO), whose first secretary-general took office in 1952. Greece and Turkey joined the alliance in 1952, West Germany in 1955. Spain became its sixteenth member in May 1982, but in December 1982 a new Spanish government indicated that the question of Spain's membership would be re-examined and might be submitted to a referendum.

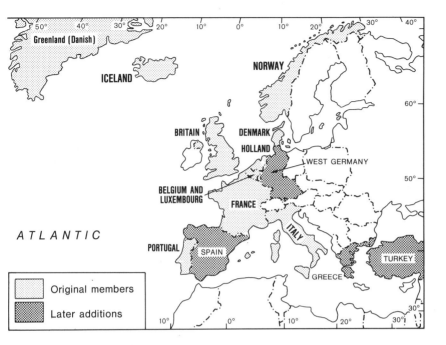

France withdrew its forces from NATO command in 1966 – without withdrawing from the treaty of alliance – and the headquarters of NATO and of its European command were then moved from France to Belgium. The disputes between Greece and Turkey (*26*) affected their participation in NATO activities in the 1970s, and Greek forces were withheld from the NATO command structure from 1974 to 1980. Although various other disputes arose between the allies from time to time, the most serious ones being those that divided the EEC members (*19*) from the United States, disturbing Soviet actions periodically reminded them of their need for the alliance.

21 Scandinavia

Traditional Scandinavian neutrality was shattered by Russia's invasion of Finland in 1939 and Nazi Germany's occupation of Denmark and Norway in 1940. The Finns, hoping to regain the territory Russia had seized (*14*), joined the Germans in attacking it in 1941. Only Sweden remained neutral throughout the 1939–45 war.

After 1945 the Scandinavians tried to restore and expand their old ties. They set up a Nordic Council for regular consultation between ministers and members of parliament from Denmark, Finland, Iceland, Norway and Sweden. A Scandinavian defence union was proposed in the late 1940s; but Denmark, Iceland and Norway, fearing that this would not give them enough security, joined the North Atlantic alliance in 1949 (*20*).

Postwar Scandinavian fears arose largely from Russia's annexation of Estonia, Latvia, Lithuania and northern East Prussia and its grip on Poland and East Germany (*14, 16, 18*). The south-eastern shores of the Baltic thus all came under Soviet control. In the far north, Russia annexed Finland's only Arctic port, Petsamo (now Pechenga), thereby reaching the Norwegian frontier; and it built up large armed forces in the Kola peninsula (*22*). In 1956 the Russians handed back Porkkala, the base west of Helsinki which they had occupied in 1944. But they had taken from Finland an eighth of all its territory; and the treaty which they signed in 1948 with a somewhat reluctant Finland obliged the Finns to help resist any future attempt to attack Russia across their territory.

In 1968–70 there were talks about forming a Nordic economic union (Nordek), but these were suspended when Soviet objections obliged Finland to drop out. Finland was, however, able to become an associate member of EFTA and, like other EFTA countries, to make a free trade agreement with the EEC in 1972 (*19*). Denmark joined the EEC in 1973, but retained its place in the Nordic Council and other Scandinavian arrangements for group co-operation. The self-governing Faroe islands stayed out of the EEC when Denmark joined, and Greenland, which obtained self-government in 1979, voted to leave the EEC in a 1982 referendum.

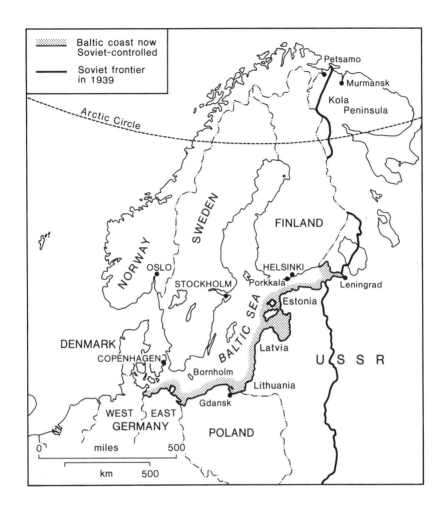

Baltic coast now
Soviet-controlled

Soviet frontier
in 1939

Arctic Circle

Petsamo

Murmansk

Kola
Peninsula

NORWAY

SWEDEN

FINLAND

OSLO

STOCKHOLM

HELSINKI

Porkkala

Leningrad

Estonia

BALTIC SEA

Latvia

DENMARK

COPENHAGEN

Bornholm

Lithuania

Gdansk

U S S R

WEST
GERMANY

EAST

POLAND

0   miles   500

km   500

22 Northern seas

The coastal states around the North Sea have shared out the rights to its seabed oil and gas by drawing dividing lines mainly based on equidistance from coasts, on the authority of the 1958 international convention on the 'continental shelf' (6). Britain – largely thanks to its Shetland and Orkney islands – and Norway got most of the oil. West Germany was initially given a very small sector, but in 1969 it obtained a ruling from the International Court at The Hague which obliged the Danes and the Dutch to cede parts of their sectors. Later, Britain and France adopted a dividing line running down the Channel, with the British Channel Islands in a small sea enclave on the French side of the line. Disputes continued about the British–Irish dividing lines. The Irish argued that baselines should not be drawn from some small islands, and particularly not from the Rockall islet, which is uninhabitable but has been formally annexed by Britain. (Denmark, meanwhile, advanced a claim that Rockall was an extension of the Faroes.)

The continental shelf is wide in this whole region; it underlies large areas west and north of Britain and Ireland as well as the whole of the North Sea. But the shelf convention did not resolve disputes over fishing rights. In the 1950s and 1960s Norway and Iceland, whose coastal fisheries had been much used by British and other trawlers, widened their fishing limits, setting off a series of disputes.

These quarrels affected Iceland's attitude to NATO, which it had joined as a founder member in 1949 (20). In 1956 it asked the Americans to withdraw from the NATO air base at Keflavik, near Reykjavik; but after long negotiations it was agreed that the base should be retained. (Keflavik's special value to NATO was that aircraft flying from it could keep watch on Soviet naval movements into the Atlantic from Murmansk – 11). Iceland extended its fishing limits to 50 miles from shore in 1972 and to 200 miles in 1975, and had several (bloodless) 'cod wars' with Britain, whose fishing fleet was hard hit by the loss of access to Icelandic and Norwegian waters.

In the mid-1970s more and more states claimed mineral and fishing rights in 200-mile-wide 'exclusive economic zones' (EEZs – 6) along their coasts. The member states of the EEC (19) proclaimed a joint EEZ.

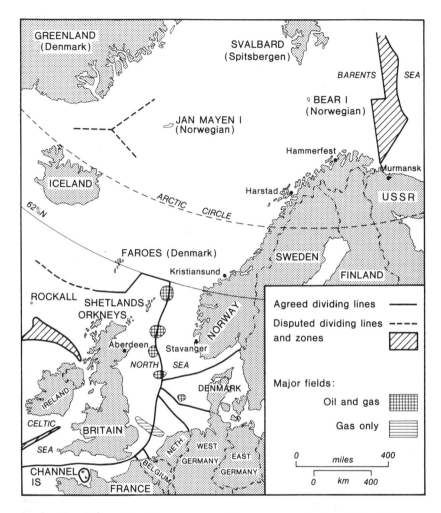

In the North Sea, this joint zone roughly corresponded to all the 'oil sectors' combined, except Norway's. Thus the greater part of the zone and of the stocks of fish in it were 'contributed' by Britain, which inevitably rejected the EEC's original (pre-EEZ) idea that all its member states should be free to fish anywhere in its waters. Wrangling among EEC members over fishing quotas, conservation and policing continued into the 1980s.

Farther north, when Norway announced a 200-mile zone for its Jan Mayen Island, disputes about dividing lines arose with Denmark (because of Greenland – *21*) and with Iceland. Norway had a more serious dispute with the USSR over the dividing line in the Barents Sea, which is rich in fish and may prove rich in oil. Norway proposed a median line, based on equidistance from coasts. The Russians argued that, for this Arctic 'sector' boundary, lines of longitude should be used. The difference involved an area of 60,000 square miles.

The Russians also rejected Norway's claim that its 'shelf' zone extended to Svalbard (Spitsbergen). Under a 1920 treaty Svalbard was recognized to be Norwegian territory, but other countries were given the right to exploit its resources on the basis of equal access under Norwegian law; both Norway and Russia mine coal there. The USSR has argued that Svalbard has its own continental shelf, whose seabed resources (which may include oil) should be accessible to all signatories of the 1920 treaty.

In the late 1940s the Russians had tried to put pressure on Norway to get it to let them put a garrison in Svalbard. Norway has kept a cautious eye on their mining camps for fear that they might create a military presence there. The USSR, for its part, has had strategic motives for discouraging other countries' activities in the Barents Sea. It wants to keep foreigners well away from its naval bases around Murmansk in the Kola peninsula. Its warships and missile-firing submarines can enter the Atlantic without having to pass through the Baltic or Mediterranean by using these bases, which are ice-free (*10*, *11*) – the effect of the Gulf Stream and its continuation in the North Atlantic Drift being to extend ice-free water far north of the Arctic Circle in these northern seas.

23 Minorities and micro-states

Some of western Europe's linguistic minority problems and separatist demands have given rise to large-scale violence, others to mainly political action – although extremist groups have turned to violence on the fringes of many non-violent political movements.

Belgium is a nation almost equally divided into two language groups. Flemish, a variant of Dutch, is mainly spoken north of a line running just south of the (bilingual) capital, Brussels. French is mainly spoken in the south, which is sometimes called Wallonia. French was historically dominant; but the Walloons are outnumbered, and Flemish dominance has been increased by the shift of economic power to the north. Constitutional changes in the 1970s introduced wide regional autonomy, but this did not end the friction, and separatist aims are still voiced by some Flemings and some Walloons.

In *Britain*, Scottish and Welsh nationalists made headway in parliamentary elections in the 1960s and 1970s. Proposals for devolution, with a separate assembly for each country, were put to referendums in 1979. The voting was negative in Wales and indecisive in Scotland, and the proposals lapsed. But nationalist agitation continued, the Welsh movement focusing on language rights, while some Scottish nationalists had North Sea oil (*22*) in mind. The Channel Islands and the Isle of Man have long enjoyed autonomy. (For *Ireland* see *24*.)

In *France*, sometimes violent agitation for autonomy or separation has developed in Brittany and Corsica, and the traditionally centralized French administrative system has also provoked unrest in the Languedoc area in the south. In 1982 a regional assembly was elected in Corsica, and the French government planned to give all regions similar assemblies as part of a general programme of decentralization. The Basques in France had not shown much discontent with their own situation, but they had been affected by the struggles of their fellow Basques in Spain.

In *Spain*, former regional rights were suppressed during General Franco's long dictatorship, and a violent nationalist movement developed in the Basque provinces. After Franco's death in 1975 there were mounting demands for decentralization, and a plan for regional autonomy was adopted, starting with the Basque provinces and Catalonia, which elected assemblies in 1980; but some Basque groups aiming at complete independence continued their terrorist activities.

Switzerland is a federation in which the 23 cantons have wide autonomy, and this has helped to reduce friction between the German-speaking majority and the minorities who speak French and Italian. However, in the 1950s agitation mounted in the French-speaking Jura district, which since 1815 had been included in the German-speaking canton of Berne. This eventually led to the creation of a separate Jura canton in 1978.

Italy now has a system of regional autonomy. A special problem on its northern border has been the German-speaking minority in the area which, before 1918, was part of Austria as South Tirol, but was called Alto Adige when it was transferred to Italy. Two-thirds of the people of Bolzano (Bozen) province speak German. In the 1950s Bolzano was joined with Trento to form a region that had an Italian-speaking majority; this set off a long agitation, which included some terrorist violence and caused friction between Italy and Austria. The two governments agreed in 1969 to settle the problem, and in 1972 Bolzano was given separate autonomy.

Luxembourg, a grand duchy with 370,000 people, has three languages, French, German and its own dialect. The map of western Europe shows several even smaller but long-established states, with populations in the 20,000 to 32,000 range: Andorra, Liechtenstein, Monaco and San Marino (there is also the tiny Vatican City state in Rome). These are all sovereign states, but they have economic and other links with larger neighbours – Luxembourg with Belgium, Andorra with both France and Spain, Liechtenstein with Switzerland, Monaco with France, San Marino and the Vatican state with Italy.

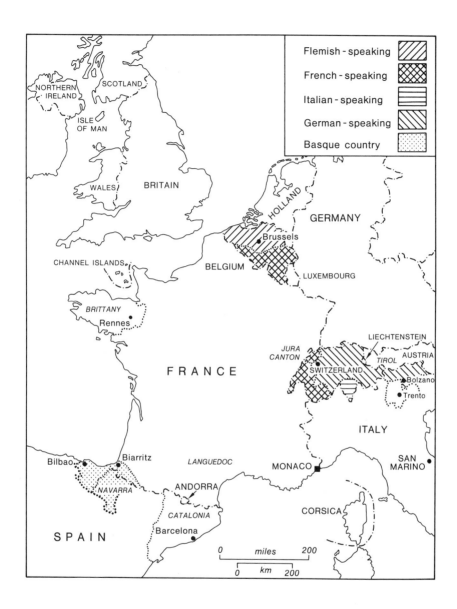

Flemish - speaking	▨
French - speaking	▩
Italian - speaking	▤
German - speaking	▨
Basque country	▨

NORTHERN
IRELAND

SCOTLAND

ISLE
OF MAN

WALES

BRITAIN

HOLLAND

GERMANY

Brussels

CHANNEL ISLANDS

BELGIUM

LUXEMBOURG

BRITTANY
Rennes

LIECHTENSTEIN

JURA
CANTON

AUSTRIA

TIROL

F R A N C E

SWITZERLAND

Bolzano

Trento

ITALY

Bilbao

Biarritz

LANGUEDOC

MONACO

SAN
MARINO

NAVARRA

ANDORRA

CATALONIA

CORSICA

S P A I N

Barcelona

0   miles   200

0   km   200

24 Ireland

The state that is usually called Britain, for short, in this book, is formally the United Kingdom of Great Britain and Northern Ireland. It was the UK of Great Britain and Ireland from 1801 until, after a bloody guerrilla war in Ireland, it was partitioned by the 1921 treaty. That treaty gave effective independence to the greater part of Ireland – which was later, in 1949, declared a republic – but it left six counties of the old northern province of Ulster in the UK, with a 'home-rule' system and a Northern Ireland parliament at Stormont in Belfast.

Successive governments in Dublin reaffirmed the aim of uniting Ireland, and the republic's constitution asserted a claim to the whole island. But the Protestant two-thirds of Northern Ireland's population of 1.5 million wished (and showed it by their voting in each election) to remain in the UK, and had no wish to be taken over by the republic, whose population (3.2 million) is now almost wholly Catholic, and whose main historical traditions are ones of usually oppressive British rule and resistance to it.

As the 1921 partition had left a large Catholic minority in Northern Ireland, politics there took a communal form, and the dominant Protestants resorted to 'gerrymandering' to control local councils in places with Catholic majorities, such as Londonderry. However, movement across the border, and between Ireland and Britain, was unrestricted; Irish migration to Britain continued; at times, too (as in 1954–62), the 'Irish Republican Army' (IRA) and other terrorist groups mounted campaigns of armed raiding into 'the north' from bases in 'the south'.

In 1965–68 the prime ministers in Dublin and Belfast joined in trying to improve north–south relations, despite opposition from extremists on both sides. Britain, which in 1965 made a free trade agreement with the republic, supported these moves for reconciliation. But a sharp backlash in 1969 led to violent communal clashes in Belfast and other northern towns, and British troops were sent to help restore peace in Northern Ireland, whose own police force had failed to protect Catholics against Protestant attacks. The IRA and similar groups regained strength. Sectarian violence recurred throughout the 1970s, with over 2000 killings.

Border of the old
province of ULSTER

Glasgow

Londonderry

NORTHERN

IRELAND

Belfast

Craigavon

Isle of
Man

Liverpool

Dublin

Shannon

REPUBLIC

OF

IRELAND

Limerick

Cork

Cardiff

0   miles   100

0   km   100

In 1982 a large British military force still remained in Northern Ireland, and the IRA's supporters depicted it as an imperialist occupying army, although most Ulster people feared what might happen if the troops were withdrawn. The province was no longer being run by its own Protestant politicians from Stormont; it was being governed from London, much like the other parts of the UK, and this improved the Catholic minority's position. But the extension of IRA terrorism to Britain had caused unease among the millions of Irish living there; and any prospect of all-Ireland unity being achieved had been set back a long way by the years of violence.

25 Gibraltar

For $2\frac{1}{2}$ centuries Gibraltar was one of Britain's most valuable naval bases. When the Suez route became a British imperial lifeline, Gibraltar and Malta were important staging posts along it (*41*). Malta, with about 350,000 people, became independent in 1964 and the last British forces left it in 1979 (*38*). For Gibraltar, however, independence did not seem a practical goal. Although its population was larger than that of such micro-states as Andorra or San Marino (*23*), it was only a narrow 4-mile-long peninsula, dominated by the spectacular Rock, and also overshadowed by Spain's recurring demands for it.

Captured by Britain in 1704 (and later renounced by Spain, in exchange for Florida), Gibraltar was thus held by Britain longer than it had been held by Spain, which had not taken it from the Moors until 1462. After 1964, when the Gibraltarians were given fuller internal self-government, Spain began to try to force them to accept its rule. It barred trade, threatened interference with air and sea routes, obstructed and later (from 1969) completely stopped border crossings. The Gibraltarians were not cowed; in a 1967 referendum they rejected Spain's claims, voting almost unanimously to retain their links with Britain, and they confirmed this decision by their votes in each subsequent election for their House of Assembly. Gibraltar's economy suffered from the 'siege', but the adjacent part of Spain was much harder hit by it.

General Franco, the dictator who imposed the 'siege', died in 1975, but it was still in force in 1982, mainly because of the Spanish army's pressure on subsequent elected governments in Madrid. In December 1982 a new Spanish government allowed border crossings for Spaniards and Gibraltarians under tightly restrictive conditions, but the economic effects of the 'siege' continued.

While Spain claimed that a foreign enclave on its coast was not tolerable, it took the opposite line on the coast of Morocco, where it held two enclaves, Ceuta and Melilla – the last remaining parts of Africa still ruled by a European state (*39*).

69

26 Cyprus, Greece and Turkey

Cyprus was ruled by Turkey from 1570 to 1878, then by Britain until 1960, but four-fifths of its 500,000 people were Greek. In 1960 it became independent with a constitution that gave the Turkish minority a share of power. Britain retained two sovereign base areas; Greece and Turkey kept small forces in Cyprus; all three countries had the right, by treaty, to intervene to maintain Cyprus's constitutional arrangements. The constitution broke down, fighting spread, and the Turkish Cypriots were driven into small enclaves. In 1964 war between Greece and Turkey seemed imminent, and a United Nations force manned by seven nations (including Britain) was installed in Cyprus. For ten years the UN men prevented clashes from escalating, but talks about a settlement became deadlocked and the Turks stayed in their enclaves, which included the northern half of Nicosia.

In 1974 the military regime which had ruled Greece since 1967 organized a military coup in Cyprus with the aim of uniting it with Greece. Turkish forces then occupied the north of the island. Greek and Turkish Cypriots fled or were driven across the new dividing line until hardly any Turks remained in the south or Greeks in the north. In Greece the military regime collapsed and democracy was restored. The Greek Cypriots' former government was also restored; and the Turkish Cypriots set up a government in the north.

The UN policed a buffer zone between the two sides but could not get them to agree on a settlement. The Greek Cypriot leaders wanted a united Cyprus, the Turkish ones a loose federation. Turkey's troops remained in northern Cyprus, whose links with the mainland grew closer.

In the Aegean Sea, Greece holds most of the islands that lie along Turkey's coast. Disputes over sea claims in the Aegean have caused several recent crises in Greek–Turkish relations. Turkey would have little freedom of movement in the Aegean or access to its fisheries and oil potential if Greece were to obtain 12-mile territorial waters and full continental shelf and 'EEZ' rights for all its islands (6).

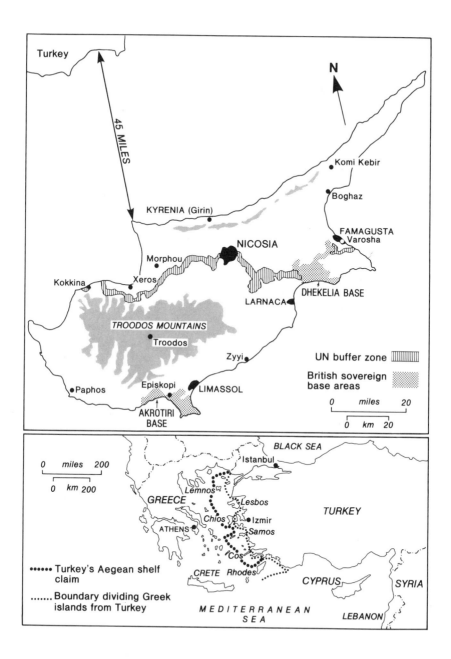

Turkey

N

45 MILES

Komi Kebir

Boghaz

KYRENIA (Girin)

FAMAGUSTA
Varosha

NICOSIA

Morphou

Kokkina   Xeros

DHEKELIA BASE

LARNACA

TROODOS MOUNTAINS
Troodos

Zyyi

UN buffer zone

British sovereign
base areas

0   miles   20

0   km   20

Paphos   Episkopi   LIMASSOL

AKROTIRI
BASE

0   miles   200

0   km 200

BLACK SEA

Istanbul

GREECE

Lemnos

Lesbos

TURKEY

Chios   Izmir

ATHENS   Samos

Cos

•••••• Turkey's Aegean shelf
         claim

CRETE   Rhodes

CYPRUS

SYRIA

.... Boundary dividing Greek
         islands from Turkey

MEDITERRANEAN
SEA

LEBANON

71

27 Asia and Africa

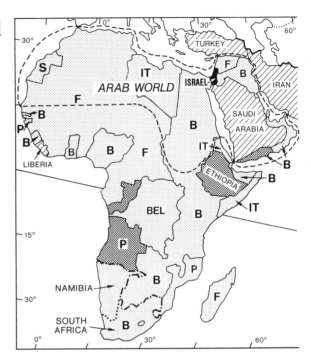

The map of these two continents has been transformed since 1945 by a rapid process of 'decolonization'. Before the 1939–45 war there were only a dozen sovereign states in the Afro-Asian world; now there are almost 100. Only a few small vestiges remain of the colonial empires that had been created by west European countries since the Portuguese first penetrated the Indian Ocean region in the 1490s. The building up of those empires had taken about 400 years, but they vanished in less than 40 years. Although their ending followed long and bloody struggles in some places, the most remarkable thing about this uniquely big and swift change in the world's map was that the transfer of power was made by negotiation and without war in the majority of the former colonies and dependencies.

The greater part of the change was in fact carried out within less than 20 years – between 1947, when India and Pakistan became independent, and 1966, when Botswana and Lesotho joined the still growing number of sovereign Commonwealth member states (9). But Portugal, the original pioneer among the west European empire-builders in Asia and Africa,

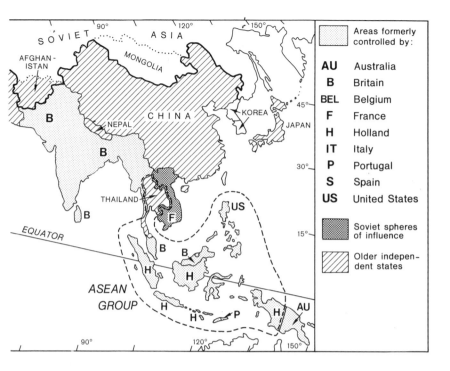

was the slowest of them to relinquish its hold, and did not concede independence to any of its territories until after its own 1974 revolution.

Only one European power, Russia, has retained control of a large area in Asia. During the 19th century the tsarist Russian empire had pushed its frontiers southward by conquering independent Moslem states in Central Asia and, farther east, taking territory from China. Its Soviet successors retained these areas, and later took effective control of (nominally independent) Mongolia and Afghanistan (*49, 53*). Russia also acquired a sphere of influence in Indochina, where in the early 1980s the Vietnamese communists had become heavily dependent on Soviet support for their occupation of Cambodia (Kampuchea) and their defiance of China (*60, 61*). Several African countries, notably Ethiopia (*35*), had by then come to rely on Russian military aid or accepted strong Russian influence.

The majority of the newly independent African and Asian states' governments had declared themselves to be 'non-aligned', as between the west and the Soviet block (*7*). But, although most of them had condemned Russia's invasion of Afghanistan, they were more often preoccupied with issues that divided them from the west – such as the terms of trade between 'north' and 'south', and the continued existence of the last remnants of west European colonialism (*41*). There was particular resentment, among the Arab states, at each sign of western support for Israel (*42–44*); among the African states, at each sign of western support for South Africa's white rulers (*33*). In the Far East, however, the five-nation ASEAN group (Association of South East Asian Nations) tended to look for western support against possible pressure from either Vietnam or China (*59*); Japan maintained many links with the west; and even China had sought to use the west as a counterweight against Soviet pressure.

A 'summit' conference of Asian and African states (including China, but not Japan) was held in 1955 at Bandung in Indonesia, but an attempt to hold one at Algiers in 1965 was something of a fiasco; too many conflicting interests had emerged in the expanded group. The majority of these states, however, joined the non-aligned movement founded in 1961, and on many economic and other issues they formed a reasonably united group in the UN assembly. They could command a majority there, whenever they did unite, from the mid-1960s onward (*8*).

28 Islam

The Moslem religion originated in Arabia, and was first spread by Arab conquests 1300 years ago. Its scriptures are in Arabic, and its holiest shrine is at Mecca, in Saudi Arabia, to which multitudes of Moslems make the pilgrimage (*haj*) every year. But the great majority of the world's 800 million Moslems are not Arabs. There are, for instance, far more Moslems in India, Pakistan and Bangladesh than in all the Arab countries put together. Moreover, not all Arabs are Moslems. There are large Christian communities in Egypt – mainly Copts – and in Lebanon – mainly Maronites.

The countries where Moslems are in a majority range from Senegal in West Africa to Indonesia in the Far East. There are also reckoned to be more than 40 million Moslems in the USSR and about 30 million in China. In the Central Asian regions of those two countries, the Moslem communities are still important and distinctive in spite of the official imposing of Marxist beliefs. The Soviet authorities have shown concern about the rapid growth in numbers of the Moslem peoples in the USSR, who now form a sixth of its whole population and, at present rates of increase, may form about a quarter of it by the year 2000 (*15*).

In historical perspective, the power of Islam was at its greatest height in the days when Moslem rulers controlled the Balkans, southern Russia, all of Central Asia and nearly all of India – before the expansion of European, Russian and Chinese power. But there has recently been a marked resurgence of Islam's importance in world affairs. Many of the new sovereign states that emerged from the old west European empires in Asia and Africa (*27*) were peopled and ruled by Moslems. The oil crises of the 1970s gave new international leverage to several Arab and other Moslem or partly Moslem states (*3, 40*). And in some areas Moslem religious fundamentalism – sometimes allied with radical political forces, sometimes competing with them for power – has revived strongly, often in reaction against modernizing policies which were regarded as alien 'westernizing' ones. A dramatic example of this was the 1979 revolution in Iran (*47*).

The Islamic Conference, an organization of governments founded in 1969, had 42 member states by 1982. Most of them could unite, at least in

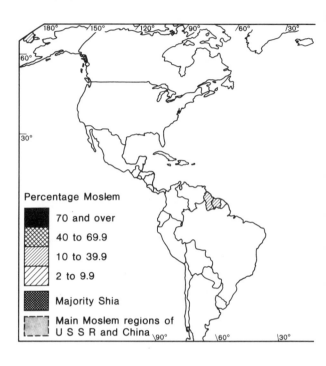

Percentage Moslem

70 and over

40 to 69.9

10 to 39.9

2 to 9.9

Majority Shia

Main Moslem regions of U S S R and China

principle, on such policies as supporting the Palestinian Arabs against Israel and the Afghan guerrillas against the Russian occupying army (*42, 43, 49*). But the war between Iran and Iraq – two members of the organization – had alarmed and divided the other members and continued in spite of their attempts at mediation; and some of them were worried about the way that such members as Libya and Iran tried to use Islamic appeals to enlarge their spheres of influence (*37, 47*).

Like other religions, Islam has its sectarian divisions. The most important one has for centuries divided the Shias (about 90 million) from the orthodox Sunni majority. The Shias are the majority group in Iran, Iraq, Oman and (North) Yemen; the 25 million of them in Pakistan and Afghanistan form important minorities, as do the Shias in some of the small Gulf states (*46*) and in Lebanon (*44*). In Syria, although the Sunnis are in a majority, the present rulers are mainly Shias of the Alawi sect. In Iraq, although the Shias are in a majority, the present rulers are mainly Sunnis; and they have long feared the spread of Shia influence from Iran, which has been a stronghold of Shia power for four centuries and, since

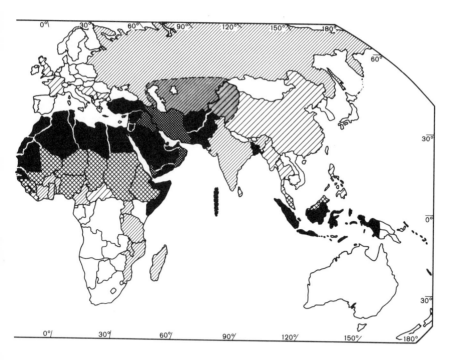

1979, has been controlled by fanatical fundamentalists. Similar fears have emerged among the Gulf states' Sunni rulers.

In the modern world of Islam, fanatical fundamentalism is not a Shia or Iranian monopoly. Several Arab governments have had cause to fear the Moslem Brotherhood, an organization which was originally founded in Egypt in 1928; the employment of fanatical assassins has been favoured by the 'Islamic socialist' rulers of Libya since its 1969 revolution; and in Malaysia the practice of basing governments on an alliance between parties representing the Chinese and Indian minorities as well as the Malays has produced, among some Malays, a backlash in the form of revived Islamic fundamentalism.

In the Americas, it is only in some small Caribbean states that immigration from India and Indonesia has produced concentrations of Moslems. However, a recent phenomenon in the USA has been the rising number of black Moslems, converted to Islam at least partly as a result of disillusion caused by many white Christians' racial prejudices.

29 The Arab world

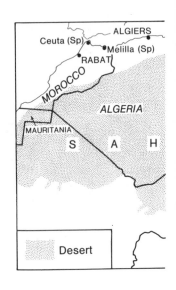

The Arabic language links 170 million people, inhabiting a belt that runs from the Atlantic to the Indian Ocean. The great majority of Arabs are Moslems, and Mecca, Islam's holiest place, is in Saudi Arabia (*28*). Modern Arab nationalism has a religious aspect, but it has mainly been a common reaction against alien rule – first by the old Turkish empire and then by west Europeans – and, since 1948, against the creation and maintenance of a Jewish state, Israel, at a central position in the Arab world. A shared nationalism has not prevented the Arab states from quarrelling among themselves: over border disputes and other local matters; over ideology (most Arab regimes have either declared themselves 'revolutionary' or taken a strongly conservative line); or when one Arab state's claims to predominance alarmed others.

The League of Arab States (or Arab League) was founded in 1945 by Egypt, Iraq, Jordan, Lebanon, Saudi Arabia, Syria and (North) Yemen. By 1982 it had been joined by Algeria, Bahrain, Djibouti, Kuwait, Libya, Mauritania, Morocco, Oman, Qatar, Somalia, Sudan, Tunisia, the United Arab Emirates and South Yemen; the Palestine Liberation Organization (*42*) was also a member. Within the League there had been much shifting of alignments, and the member states' relative influence had been strongly affected by the new wealth that some of them obtained from their oilfields (*40*). Several attempts at uniting two or more states had been made. In 1958 Egypt and Syria formed the United Arab

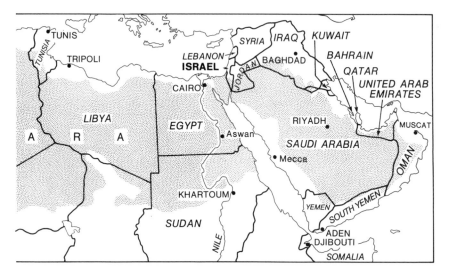

Republic; Syria broke away in 1961, but Egypt remained officially known as the UAR until 1971. In 1971–72 the seven small Gulf states formerly known as the Trucial States (or Trucial Oman) formed the United Arab Emirates (UAE – *46*).

No clear line marks the Arab world's southern border in Africa. Djibouti, Mauritania and Somalia have joined the Arab League, and Arabic is widely used in those three states, but they have not normally been regarded as Arab states in the past.

30 Africa

In Africa, both European colonization and decolonization were rapid (*27*). Until the 'scramble for Africa' in the 1880s, Europeans had controlled only a few coastal strips, and some areas in the extreme north and south (*33, 38*). Then, within one century, nearly all of Africa came under European rule and re-emerged from it. In Algeria, the Portuguese-held territories and Rhodesia long guerrilla wars preceded their liberation; most of the other new states attained independence more peacefully. By 1980, white rule in 'black Africa' was limited to South Africa and Namibia. Djibouti, the last territory held by a European power, had been given its independence by France in 1977 (*35*); Rhodesia had become black-ruled Zimbabwe (*32*). North of the Sahara, Spain still held two small enclaves on the coast of Morocco (*39*).

Communications within Africa are impeded by the deserts, dense forests and lack of navigable rivers. Several hundred languages are spoken, and many of the new states, whose frontiers were marked out by the European colonizers, have to contend with antagonisms between tribes, of the kind that have marked the conflicts in Nigeria, Chad, Uganda and elsewhere (*34–37*). The Organization of African Unity, founded in 1963, has in general tried to discourage secessions and attempts to change frontiers by force; the predominant feeling is that, although the present frontiers cut through some tribes and group others unwillingly together, failure to uphold them would open the way to unlimited fragmentation and conflict. By 1982, however, the OAU's member governments were so sharply divided that its future seemed in doubt. The most divisive issues at the time concerned Morocco's occupation of (ex-Spanish) Western Sahara (*39*) and Libya's attempts to dominate Chad and other states south of the Sahara (*37, 38*). Libya's ambitions had aggravated tension along the line, running eastward roughly from Guinea to Somalia, that divides the Islamic north from the rest of Africa (*28*).

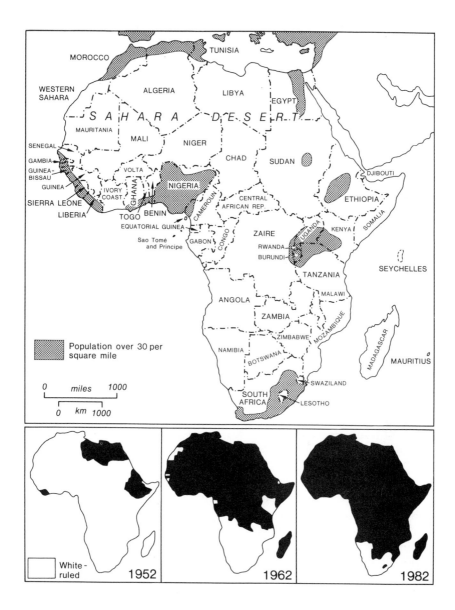

Population over 30 per square mile

0   miles   1000

0   km   1000

White-ruled   1952

1962

1982

81

31 Southern Africa

By 1962 the period of European rule had ended for most of Africa north of the Equator; but not in the southern part of the continent (*30*). In the far south lay the Republic of South Africa (RSA), ruled by its large white minority, whose influence was felt throughout the region (*33*). Portugal's government was determined to retain Angola and Mozambique and was promoting white settlement there; the number of whites in Angola had risen from 44,000 in 1940 to about 200,000 in 1960; the Portuguese garrisons were being increased to deal with the guerrilla war which African liberation movements had started in Angola in 1961. Southern Rhodesia (now Zimbabwe), nominally a British colony, was in practice ruled by its small white minority; the original white settlement there in the 1890s had been made from South Africa, whose influence on the Rhodesian whites was stronger than Britain's.

The mineral wealth of southern Africa was one cause of the creation there of large white communities. Another was the existence of healthy highland areas suitable for growing commercial crops (e.g. coffee in Kenya, tobacco in Rhodesia).

North of the RSA, the whites' domination was gradually overcome. A turning point was seen in 1963: Kenya became independent (*35*); the white-backed secession of Zaire's mineral-rich Katanga province (now Shaba) was ended by UN action; Britain dissolved the Central African Federation established in 1953 (*32*). Africans had come to regard that federation merely as a means for Southern Rhodesia's whites to extend their control over Northern Rhodesia and Nyasaland – which, as Zambia and Malawi, became independent in 1964.

In 1965 Southern Rhodesia's whites declared it independent. With help from the RSA they defied international economic sanctions; but African guerrilla resistance to their regime grew, its position was weakened when Angola and Mozambique became independent in 1975, and in 1980 a new black government of Zimbabwe took over (*32*). Meanwhile the RSA was being pressed to concede independence to Namibia (*34*).

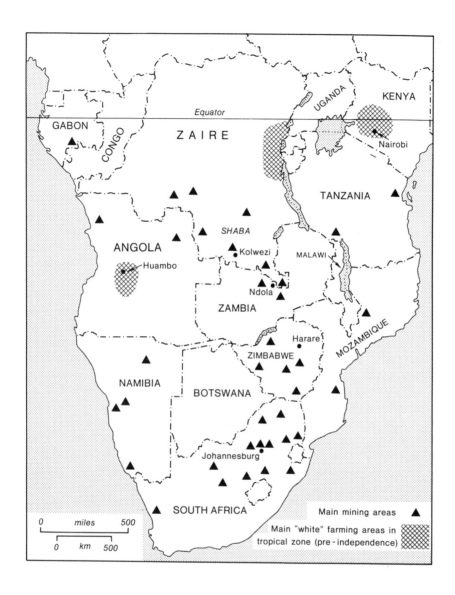

GABON

CONGO

ZAIRE

Equator

UGANDA

KENYA

Nairobi

TANZANIA

SHABA

ANGOLA

Kolwezi

MALAWI

Huambo

Ndola

ZAMBIA

MOZAMBIQUE

Harare

ZIMBABWE

NAMIBIA

BOTSWANA

Johannesburg

SOUTH AFRICA

| 0 | miles | 500 |
| 0 | km | 500 |

Main mining areas ▲

Main "white" farming areas in tropical zone (pre-independence)

83

32 Zaire, Zambia, Zimbabwe

Zaire has only a narrow outlet to the sea, at the Congo river mouth. Zambia, Zimbabwe and Malawi are completely landlocked (and the Zambezi and Limpopo rivers are not navigable). Mining development in these countries (*31*) was made possible by the building of railways northward from South Africa and inland from the coasts of Angola and Mozambique (both Portuguese-ruled until 1975). The landlocked states' dependence on these routes strongly influenced events from 1960 onward. A new railway, the Tanzania–Zambia (Tazara, or Tanzam) line, was built in 1970–75 with Chinese help to reduce Zambia's dependence on routes which were then still under white control.

Zaire, the former Belgian Congo, was granted independence in 1960 hastily and without any real preparation. Its troops mutinied against the Belgians who still commanded them, and anarchy spread. Belgium sent its own troops in to protect the 110,000 whites; the UN sent an international force to restore order and ensure the Belgian troops' withdrawal. But the mineral-rich province of Katanga (now Shaba) was declared a separate state under a government backed by local Belgian interests – with some support from Rhodesia and South Africa – which defied the UN with the help of white mercenaries. The central government in Leopoldville (now Kinshasa) disintegrated, and a rival regime backed by Russia was set up at Stanleyville (Kisangani). The UN helped to bring together a new national government and, in 1963, to end the Katanga secession. In 1964, after the UN force had withdrawn, a new rebellion at Stanleyville led Belgium to fly in troops to rescue hostages held there. In 1967 former mercenaries – both white and black – staged brief revolts at Bukavu and in Katanga. Black ex-mercenaries who had fled into Angola invaded Katanga (Shaba) in 1977, and again in 1978, when French and Belgian troops were flown in at Zaire's request and later replaced by an African international force.

The Zaire–Zambia frontier took its rather odd shape in the 1890s, when whites moving north from South Africa met other whites, working for the 'Congo Free State' enterprise that had been formed by King Leopold II of Belgium, who were moving south-eastwards. They drew a line that divides a region rich in copper and other minerals (*31*). The

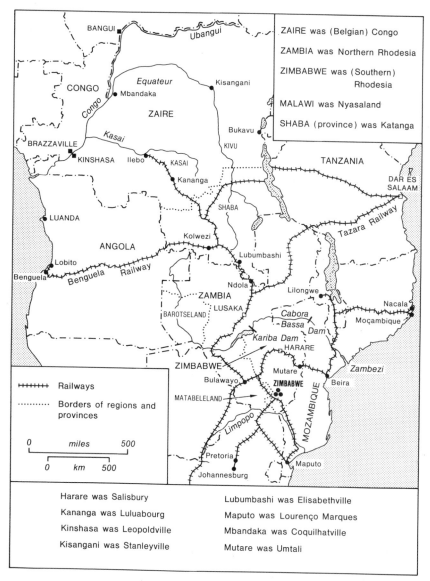

ZAIRE was (Belgian) Congo

ZAMBIA was Northern Rhodesia

ZIMBABWE was (Southern) Rhodesia

MALAWI was Nyasaland

SHABA (province) was Katanga

Railways

Borders of regions and provinces

0   miles   500

0   km   500

Harare was Salisbury

Kananga was Luluabourg

Kinshasa was Leopoldville

Kisangani was Stanleyville

Lubumbashi was Elisabethville

Maputo was Lourenço Marques

Mbandaka was Coquilhatville

Mutare was Umtali

areas south of this line were at first taken over by the British South Africa Company created by the South African millionaire, Cecil Rhodes. Later Southern Rhodesia became a self-governing (in practice, white-ruled) colony, while Northern Rhodesia, where there were fewer whites, and

Nyasaland, its neighbour to the east, were ruled as British protectorates. A federation of these three territories was formed in 1953 but dissolved in 1963. In 1964 Northern Rhodesia and Nyasaland became independent as Zambia and Malawi. But in Southern Rhodesia the whites resisted British pressure for a gradual shift of political power to the black majority. In 1965 they declared an independent republic and cut their constitutional links with Britain.

Through the UN, Britain got international trade embargoes ('sanctions') imposed on the rebellious white regime; but South Africa and, until 1974, Portugal helped its economy to keep going, and Zambia could not apply sanctions fully, because of its dependence on trade routes through Rhodesian, Portuguese and South African territory. South Africa sent forces to help the Rhodesian whites fight the African guerrillas who operated from bases in Zambia and, after 1975, in Mozambique. Rhodesian forces raided into those two countries, striking at guerrilla bases and also at Zambia's communications with Tanzania, with the aim of keeping it dependent on the routes through Rhodesia. The growing strain of sanctions and the guerrilla war led the Rhodesian whites to form, in 1978, a government in which they gave a share of power to some black leaders; but this did not bring peace. In 1980, after a cease-fire had been achieved as a result of negotiations in London, a general election held under British and Commonwealth supervision produced a new black government for what had been renamed Zimbabwe (from the site of the ancient ruins in the south-east of the country). Sanctions were ended, and Zimbabwe's independence was internationally recognized. Its remaining problems included the old antagonism between its two main tribal groups, the Mashona majority and the historically dominant Matabele (about 20% of the population), on which two rival guerrilla armies had been based. In 1982 there was widespread unrest in Matabeleland, Zimbabwe's south-western region.

After 1980 Mozambique, although freed from its involvement in the Rhodesia/Zimbabwe war, was still affected by the South African-backed MNR guerrillas' struggle against the leftist government that had been installed in Maputo in 1975. In 1982 the guerrillas were blocking the railways from Maputo to Zimbabwe and from Beira to Malawi. Zimbabwe sent troops into Mozambique to help its government to defend the railway and oil pipeline running to Zimbabwe from Beira.

33 South Africa

South Africa's population of 29 million includes $4\frac{1}{2}$ million whites, of whom over half are 'Afrikaners' (originally of Dutch origin), the others being mainly of British origin. There are 21 million black Africans; about 850,000 Indians (although immigration from India has long been halted); and $2\frac{1}{2}$ million 'Coloureds' of mixed origin: paradoxically, in this country where race segregation has in recent years been imposed more thoroughly than anywhere else in the world, past interbreeding between whites and blacks has produced a community of mixed origin which, in proportion to the white population, is uniquely large.

The first Dutch colony around Cape Town was established in 1652. Britain annexed the Cape in 1814. South Africa's history from then on comprised two long struggles: between the British and the 'Boers', between whites and blacks. The value of the prize was much increased by the discoveries, from the 1860s onward, of diamonds, gold and other minerals, especially the gold of the Rand (Witwatersrand) area around Johannesburg. By the late 1940s the Afrikaners had won both contests.

Since the 1950s, while white colonial rule has been brought to an end in other parts of the continent, an increasingly isolated South Africa has seen a tightening up of the system of repression designed to perpetuate its white minority rule. In 1961 South Africa became a republic and withdrew from the Commonwealth. In the late 1960s Britain gave independence to the three adjacent protectorates, Bechuanaland (now Botswana), Swaziland and Basutoland (now Lesotho), which South Africa had once expected to take over; but their economies remained heavily dependent on South Africa, and their new independence did not seriously affect its ruling whites' position. More serious was the loss, between 1975 and 1980, of the sheltering screen to the north that had been provided by Portugal's Angola and Mozambique colonies and by white-ruled Rhodesia (now Zimbabwe). Only one part of the former screen remained: Namibia (South-West Africa), where South Africa faced international pressure for the territory to be given its independence, and where it was also involved in a long struggle against Namibian guerrillas which had led it into a conflict with Angola (*31*, *32*, *34*).

Inside South Africa, political power was kept in the hands of the white minority; in 1982 there was discussion of proposals to let the Indians and Coloureds elect separate parliamentary chambers, but these proposals were designed to leave the whites' monopoly of real power untouched. As for the black majority, arrangements had been made to ensure that it would eventually be deprived of any claim to political rights in South Africa.

The former 'native areas' were converted, after a little consolidation, into 'homelands' ('Bantustans') for the 10 main African tribal groups. After a period of self-government, the homelands were pressed to accept 'independence'. This status brought them no real advantage, as they were not internationally recognized as independent states, and they remained completely dependent on South Africa in practice. But, when tribal homelands became 'independent', South Africa could treat all members of those tribes – even though most of them had lived for generations in 'white' areas and cities – as immigrant 'foreigners'.

By 1982, four 'independent' states had been proclaimed: Bophuthat-swana, Ciskei, Transkei and Venda. Meanwhile, more than 3 million Africans had been expelled from the 'white' areas on various pretexts and dumped into the homelands, where there was neither work nor land for them. The ultimate aim was that the black labour force on which the 'white' areas and cities depended would be permitted in those areas only as 'foreign' migrant labour, without any right of residence or claim to citizenship in South Africa; their only political rights would relate to 'homelands' which many of them would never see unless they were expelled to them. Thus, by a skilful juggling of the 'homeland' fragments on its map, South Africa would cease to have a black majority; it would be a mainly white nation that provided employment, on its own terms, for millions of black 'foreigners' whose own 'homelands' – lacking mines, cities, industries or even good farmland – could not support them.

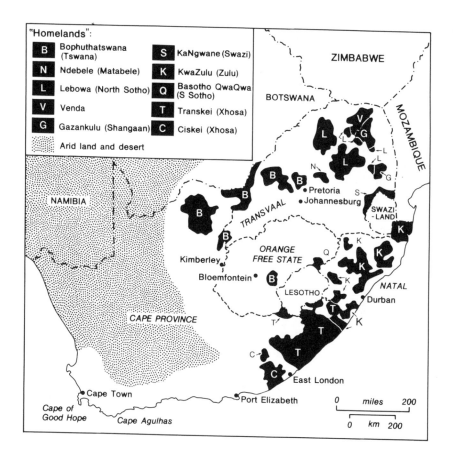

"Homelands":

B	Bophuthatswana (Tswana)	**S**	KaNgwane (Swazi)
N	Ndebele (Matabele)	**K**	KwaZulu (Zulu)
L	Lebowa (North Sotho)	**Q**	Basotho QwaQwa (S Sotho)
V	Venda	**T**	Transkei (Xhosa)
G	Gazankulu (Shangaan)	**C**	Ciskei (Xhosa)

Arid land and desert

ZIMBABWE

BOTSWANA

MOZAMBIQUE

NAMIBIA

TRANSVAAL

N

Pretoria

Johannesburg

S

SWAZI-LAND

K

ORANGE FREE STATE

Q

Kimberley

Bloemfontein

LESOTHO

NATAL

Durban

CAPE PROVINCE

K

T

East London

Cape Town

Cape of Good Hope

Cape Agulhas

Port Elizabeth

0	miles	200
0	km	200

34 Angola and Namibia

In Angola, the Portuguese withdrawal in 1975 (*31*) left three rival guerrilla movements fighting for power: the FNLA, based on the Bakongo tribes in the north; UNITA, based on the Ovimbundu, who form a third of Angola's population of 7 million; and the leftist MPLA, then strongest in coastal areas. At first the FNLA and UNITA got American backing, and South Africa sent a force to help UNITA; but Russia flew in Cuban troops to help the MPLA, which was then able to hold the capital, Luanda, and set up a government there. Resistance to the MPLA regime continued, although the FNLA lost strength, especially when Zaire expelled its leaders in 1978.

In 1982 UNITA held large areas in the south-east and could harass the Benguela railway (formerly a major outlet for the Zaire–Zambia mining region – *32*); but it had become a tool of South Africa in the conflict along the Namibia border. The government in Luanda still relied on Cuban soldiers (*70*) and followed Russia's line on international issues; but it sought western aid, and got much of its revenue from American firms operating in the coastal oilfields (mainly in Cabinda).

Namibia (South-West Africa), controlled by Germany 1884–1914 and thereafter by South Africa, is largely desert and has only one million inhabitants (including 75,000 whites); half of them are Ovambo, living near the northern border. The uranium mined at Rössing and the diamonds of the Lüderitz–Oranjemund coast are the most notable resources. Walvis Bay is legally part of South Africa. South Africa held the rest of the territory under a League of Nations mandate in the 1920s and 1930s, but later refused to place it under UN trusteeship.

After 1975 the Namibian guerrilla movement, SWAPO, was able to use bases in Angola. To counter it, South Africa deployed large forces in northern Namibia, including the Caprivi Strip (named after the minister who got Germany this 'corridor' to the Zambezi in 1890). In 1981–82 South African forces were making many raids into southern Angola, where they effectively controlled some border areas.

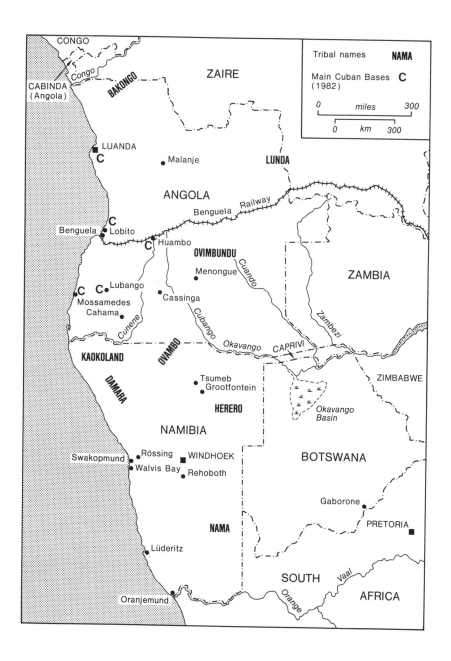

35 East Africa

Ethiopia (formerly known as Abyssinia) was conquered by Fascist Italy in 1936, but liberated by British forces in 1941. Thus, after a brief experience of European colonialism, it re-emerged as what was then Africa's only independent monarchy. Eritrea, a former Italian colony, was federated with Ethiopia in 1952. After 1962, when Ethiopia imposed its authority on Eritrea more directly, guerrilla resistance increased among the Eritreans (who are largely Moslem) and drew support from some Arab states. Fighting was still going on in Eritrea in 1982, and the guerrillas of a liberation movement in the neighbouring Tigre province were co-operating with the Eritrean ones.

Somalia, another former Italian colony, was a UN trust territory from 1946 to 1960, when it became independent, absorbing the former British Somaliland, which is now Somalia's north-western region. Many subsequent clashes in border areas resulted from nationalist stirrings among the Moslem Somalis living in eastern Kenya, in the Ogaden and Haud regions of Ethiopia, and in Djibouti (then a French territory). The Kenya–Somalia border conflicts were virtually ended by an agreement reached in 1968. Djibouti became independent in 1977, after the leaders of its Afar (Danakil) and Somali (Issa) communities had agreed to share power. It retained a small French garrison, but its relations with Somalia no longer seemed to cause anxiety. Meanwhile, Somalia's continuing feud with Ethiopia had led it to sign a defence pact with the USSR and allow the Russians to build naval and air bases on its soil.

After the 1974 military coup in Ethiopia, the Russians soon obtained an influence over its new rulers – who were young army officers bent on making revolutionary changes in a country traditionally ruled by its emperor and its feudal aristocracy, and strongly influenced by its own distinctive Christian church (although many of its inhabitants, outside the central Amharic-speaking region, were Moslems). By 1977 Soviet military support for Ethiopia had reached such a scale that Somalia expelled the Russian military missions and turned to the Americans. The Americans were willing to help Somalia defend itself, but not to help it to attack Ethiopia. Between 1977 and 1980 Somalia's forces and local Somali guerrillas tried to win control of the Ogaden but were defeated.

Many thousands of Somalis from the Ogaden became refugees in Somalia. By then Russia was providing arms for the Ethiopian forces fighting in Eritrea and Tigre as well as on the Somali front, and it had sent several thousand Cubans to fight alongside the Ethiopians.

Sudan, formerly an Anglo-Egyptian condominium (in practice ruled by the British), became independent in 1956. From then on, its black south was in revolt against the domination of the Arabized Moslem north almost continuously until 1972, when the south was granted regional autonomy. This concession brought peace. There have been large movements of refugees across Sudan's borders: first, its own southerners fleeing into neighbouring states; then, inflows from Eritrea and Ethiopia, from Uganda (see below) and Chad (37).

Kenya, Uganda, Tanganyika and Zanzibar (the last two being united in 1964 as Tanzania) had all been British-ruled before they came to independence in the early 1960s (9). For some years they went on operating many transport and other services jointly; but by 1977 the collapse of their East African Community had to be formally acknowledge. Kenya and Tanzania were so much at odds that the frontier between them had been closed. The worst trouble, however had arisen in Uganda.

Uganda became independent in 1962 with a constitution that preserved its old tribal monarchies; the most important of these was Buganda, the kingdom of the Baganda, who inhabit the region around the capital, Kampala. In 1967 President Milton Obote's government abolished the monarchies; this and other actions aroused widespread opposition. In 1971 the army commander, General Idi Amin Dada, seized power. Amin's rule proved singularly brutal. He expelled the Asian community, and his soldiers (largely recruited from a Moslem area in north-western Uganda) killed many thousands of people and imposed a reign of terror. In 1976 Amin's international notoriety was increased by the dubious role he played when Arab and German hijackers brought a planeload of hostages, including many Israelis, to the airport at Entebbe. An Israeli airborne commando rescued the Entebbe hostages.

In 1978 Amin's forces invaded Tanzania, occupying a large border area. In 1979 Tanzanian forces and armed groups of Ugandan exiles counter-attacked into Uganda. They met only limited resistance, although Libya sent troops to help Amin's, which retreated into the north-west and then fled into Zaire and Sudan. Tanzanian forces remained in Uganda until 1981; by then Obote had become president again. In 1982 there was still much disorder (largely caused by the new Ugandan army) and guerrilla resistance to the government.

Rwanda and Burundi, two small highland states, became independent in 1962 after periods of German and then Belgian rule. They had long been dominated by the distinctively tall Watutsi minority tribes. In

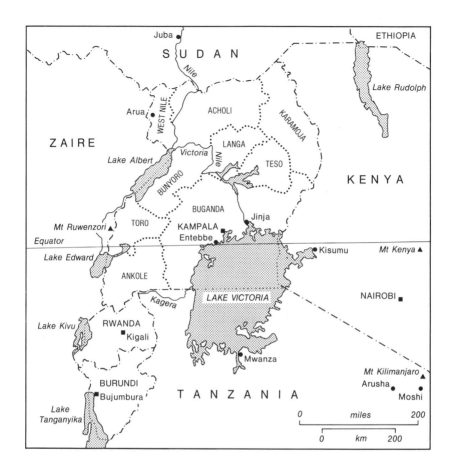

Rwanda this domination was overthrown in 1959. Burundi's Watutsi monarchy was brought to a less violent end in 1966, and the Watutsi ascendancy persisted there.

36 Nigeria and Guinea coast

Around the Gulf of Guinea, five European nations' colonial rivalries left a patchwork of frontiers. Until 1957 the region's only sovereign state was Liberia, where American-sponsored settlement of freed slaves had begun in the 1820s; but by 1975 all the colonies had become independent.

Germany's two pre-1914 colonies, Togo and Cameroon, were later each divided into British and French territories. In 1960 the French portions became independent states and, after UN-supervised plebiscites, British Togoland joined Ghana; the British Cameroons' northern part joined Nigeria; and the southern part joined (ex-French) Cameroon.

The Gambia (British until 1965) called in troops from (ex-French) Senegal to help suppress a coup in 1981; the two states then agreed to form a federation, called Senegambia. Other new names had appeared after independence. The Gold Coast became Ghana; (ex-French)

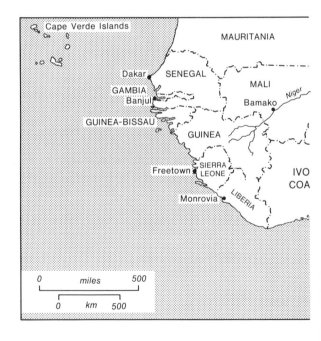

Soudan became Mali; French, Portuguese and Spanish Guinea became respectively Guinea, Guinea-Bissau and Equatorial Guinea; Dahomey renamed itself Benin (although Benin City is in Nigeria). The Gambian capital, Bathurst, became Banjul; the Chad one, Fort Lamy, became Ndjamena. Macias Nguema, who ruled Equatorial Guinea after it became independent in 1968, gave his own name to Fernando Poo island, but he was overthrown in 1979.

Nigeria, Africa's most populous country (*1*), overshadows its neighbours. It became independent in 1960 as a federation of three regions: the huge, mainly Moslem, north, with half the population; the west and the east, dominated respectively by the Yoruba and Ibo peoples. In 1966 there were two military coups, one largely inspired by Ibos, one aimed against them. In 1967 some Ibo leaders proclaimed a separate state, called Biafra. Their forces were driven back into a small south-eastern area where they held out until 1970; this civil war caused mass starvation in the Ibo area and bitter dissension among Africa's governments. In 1979 Nigeria restored civilian government and held elections; the federation had been reshaped, with 19 states replacing the three regions, and Abuja was chosen to succeed Lagos as the captial.

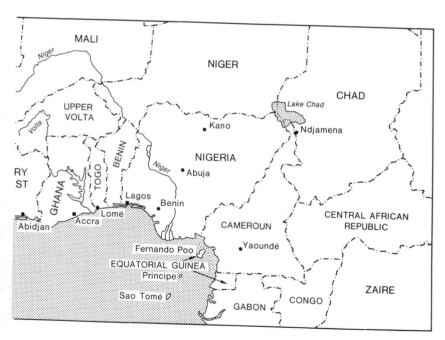

37 Ex-French Africa

France's former territories in Africa – apart from Djibouti and Madagascar (*30*) – stretched from the Mediterranean to the Congo river. In this area there are now 17 sovereign states. In the north, Morocco, Algeria and Tunisia are Arab countries (*38, 39*). The other 14 states, formerly grouped as French West and Equatorial Africa, have a combined population much smaller than Nigeria's; the Sahara Desert covers much of Mali, Niger and Chad and most of Mauritania. Guinea became independent in 1958, the other 13 in 1960. Congo has often been called Congo-Brazzaville, to distinguish it from the former Belgian Congo, now Zaire. The Central African Republic was declared an 'empire' in 1976 by its ruler, Colonel Bokassa, but he was ousted in 1979 and the CAR resumed its claim to be a republic.

Several groupings of states that appeared in the region after 1960 proved ephemeral. One that still seemed effective in 1982 was the Economic Community of West African States (ECOWAS), established in 1975; of its 16 members – Niger, Nigeria and all the states west of them – nine were ex-French. France retained influence in many of its former African dependencies, but Russia got some foothold in Benin, Congo and Guinea, and in the 1970s Mali, Niger, Upper Volta and other states were alarmed by Libya's ambitions (*38*).

Libya's most open intervention was in Chad, where factional fighting after independence – largely between southerners and Moslem northerners – repeatedly reached the scale of civil war. The Libyans took advantage of this to occupy the Aozou area in northern Chad in 1973, and in 1980 they sent 14,000 soldiers to Chad's capital, Ndjamena, drove out one of the rival forces that were fighting there, and proclaimed the union of Chad with Libya. The defeated force – led by a Moslem northerner, Hissène Habré – fell back to Chad's eastern border region and, with some support from Sudan, held out there against Libyan attacks. The factions that had welcomed the Libyan troops became disenchanted with them, the Libya–Chad union evaporated, and the OAU (*30*) pressed the Libyans to leave Chad. When they left in late 1981 a small OAU force was temporarily stationed in Chad, but by mid-1982 it had withdrawn and Hissène Habré had recaptured Ndjamena and formed a new government

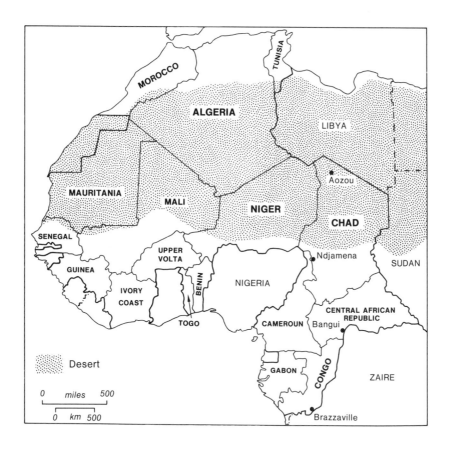

there. Libya then installed a rival government in northernmost Chad, near Aozou. This rivalry, and more general suspicions about Libya's aim of dominating the weaker states south of the Sahara, contributed to the collapse of the OAU summit conference that was to have been held in Libya in 1982; so many African heads of state stayed away that there was no quorum.

When Mauritania became independent in 1960 Morocco revived old claims on it, but these claims were abandoned in 1969 and both states then turned their attention to Western Sahara (39).

38 North Africa

In the *Maghreb* (the 'West' of the Arab world), two former French protectorates, Morocco and Tunisia, became independent in 1956 (*37, 39*); but 7 years of fighting, which engaged a large French army, preceded Algeria's achievement of independence in 1962. A million Europeans had settled in Algeria since France first colonized it in 1830; most of them left after 1962. Border disputes between Morocco and Algeria led to fighting in the 1960s. Later, another quarrel developed when Algeria provided bases and arms for the guerrillas in Western Sahara (*39*).

These countries' main culture is Arabic, but the original Berber population's language and customs survive in many places, notably in Kabylia, east of Algiers, where demands for the protection of Berber culture have been mounting.

Libya, which Italy had taken from Turkey in 1911, became independent in 1951. It has only 3 million inhabitants and is mostly desert, but in the 1960s it was enriched by its oilfields (*40*). After a military coup in 1969 Colonel Moamer Qaddafi and other officers installed an Islamic 'revolutionary' regime which used the oil revenues to pursue ambitious foreign policies. Libyan forces were sent to fight in Uganda (*35*) and Chad (*37*); Libya backed opposition groups in Tunisia, Egypt, Sudan, Somalia and several West African states (*35, 37*); its agents carried out assassinations in several European countries (*28*).

Libya's sea claims also caused tensions. In 1974 it claimed the Gulf of Sirte as 'internal waters', and in 1981 its aircraft attacked American ones above this stretch of sea. In 1980 its navy forced Malta to stop exploring for oil about 60 miles from the Maltese coast. That action ended a period during which Libya had obtained much influence in Malta, partly by providing cheap oil. Malta, independent since 1964, had seen the last British forces leave its historic naval base in 1979, and it needed substitutes for the revenue that the base had brought it; but its government reacted angrily to Libya's bullying tactics.

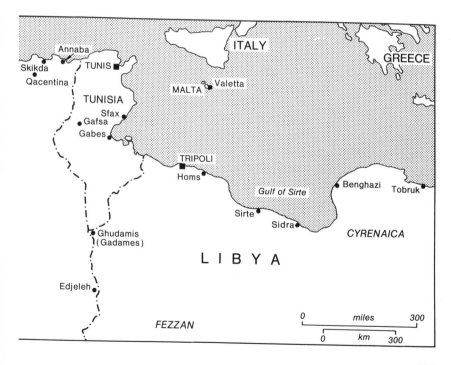

39 Morocco and Western Sahara

Before Morocco became independent in 1956 most of it had been under French control, but Spain had held zones in the north and the south, and Tangier had been an international zone. Until 1969 Spain retained an enclave at Ifni, and it still holds two '*presidios*', Ceuta and Melilla.

In 1975 Spain withdrew from its Western Sahara territory – a very thinly peopled, mainly desert area, its only notable resources being the phosphates near Bou Craa. Morocco, which had old claims to the territory, sent in troops, while Mauritania took over part of the southern region (Rio de Oro). They both met resistance from the Polisario guerrilla movement, backed by Algeria and based on the Tindouf area. In 1979 Mauritania withdrew its forces. Morocco then took over coastal positions in the south, but it could not stop the guerrillas operating in the desert interior, and in the north they even raided the Zag area in Morocco. By 1982 Morocco's forces were concentrating on keeping the Polisario ones from penetrating a fortified line which protected Bou Craa, Smara and the north-west.

Morocco had offered to hold a referendum so that the Saharans could choose between independence and attachment to Morocco; but, as some of them were refugees in Algeria and some were nomads who took little notice of frontiers, there was much dispute about how many people should be entitled to vote. Meanwhile half of the 50 African states had recognized the Saharan government-in-exile which the Polisario leaders had proclaimed. When its delegates were seated at OAU meetings many other delegates walked out in protest, and this dispute was one of the causes of the deadlock that affected OAU activities in 1982 (*30, 37*).

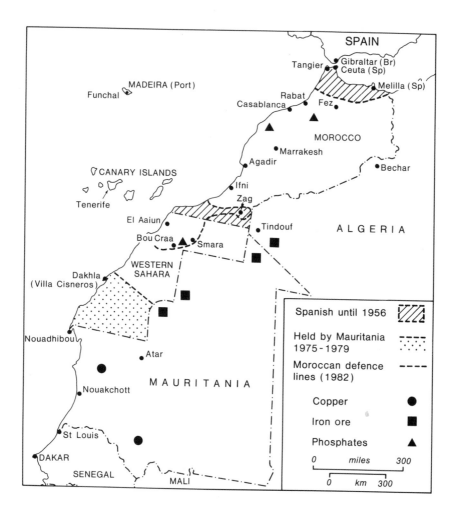

SPAIN

Tangier • Gibraltar (Br)
• Ceuta (Sp)

MADEIRA (Port)
Funchal ◦

• Melilla (Sp)

Rabat
Casablanca •
Fez •

▲

MOROCCO

• Marrakesh
Agadir •

• Bechar

▽ CANARY ISLANDS

◦ ◦

Tenerife

Ifni

Zag

El Aaiun •
• Tindouf

Bou Craa ▲ Smara

ALGERIA

■

■

WESTERN
SAHARA

Dakhla •
(Villa Cisneros)

■

■

Nouadhibou

• Atar

●

MAURITANIA

• Nouakchott

• St Louis

●

DAKAR •

SENEGAL

MALI

Spanish until 1956

Held by Mauritania
1975-1979

Moroccan defence
lines (1982)

Copper ●

Iron ore ■

Phosphates ▲

0   miles   300

0   km   300

40 Middle East and North African oil

Oil production began in Iran (Persia) in 1912. In the 1920s oilfields near Kirkuk in northern Iraq were developed. Production began in Saudi Arabia in 1939 and in Kuwait in 1945. By the mid-1950s the Middle East was producing a fifth of the world's oil, and supplying three-quarters of western Europe's needs. The Arab countries of North Africa then also began to produce oil (and Algeria developed a big export trade in natural gas too). The Middle East and North African oil-exporting states – all of them Arab states, except Iran – were producing a quarter of the world's output in 1960; by 1970 they were producing two-fifths of it. Much of this oil came from desert areas, and the wealth it brought transformed the position of countries such as Saudi Arabia and Libya.

The oilfields were originally developed by western companies – American, British, French and Dutch in Iraq, American and British in Kuwait, American in Saudi Arabia. In 1951 the British company working in Iran was expropriated and its refinery at Abadan was seized.

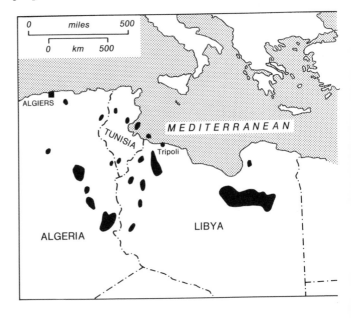

Thereafter, the exporting states took an increasingly tight grip on the industry, raising taxes, nationalizing some firms, setting stiffer terms for others, and creating their own state oil corporations. But the region's oil, being plentiful and accessible (even the offshore fields in the Gulf are in relatively shallow water), remained cheap enough to take a growing share of the world market.

Pipelines were built to carry some Iraqi and Saudi oil to ports on the Mediterranean, but most oil from the Gulf region went by tanker from Gulf ports even before the flow through the pipelines was affected by successive conflicts involving Syria, Lebanon and Israel. Tankers bound for Europe mostly used the Suez Canal until it, too, was affected by the region's conflicts; but when it was closed in 1967 (42) the longer 'Cape route' around South Africa had to be used, and bigger tankers were built to make that route more economic. The oil traffic did not all return to the Suez Canal when it was reopened in 1975 and deepened and widened in 1980. Meanwhile, alternative 'short-cuts' emerged. When Israel opened a pipeline from Eilat (42) to the Mediterranean in 1970, it could not expect Arab governments to approve of Arab oil passing through it; but in 1977 Egypt opened the 'Sumed' pipeline, running from south of Suez to a point on the Mediterranean near Alexandria, and by 1981 there was also a new pipeline crossing Saudi Arabia to a port near Medina.

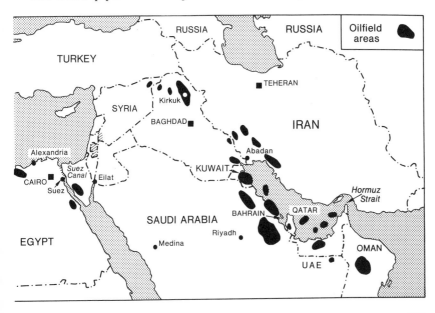

Eight of the 13 members of the Organization of Petroleum Exporting Countries (OPEC) are in the Middle East and North Africa. The Arab states also have their own grouping, OAPEC. Saudi Arabia is much the biggest producer in OPEC, and the conflicts in the Middle East have had dramatic effects on the world's oil market and on its whole economy (*3, 43, 47*). Although the OPEC cartel's power and the effectiveness of what has been called 'the Arab oil weapon' had been reduced by 1982, the Middle East and North Africa still contained three-fifths of the world's known reserves of oil – Saudi Arabia alone containing a quarter.

The proximity of Russia to the oil-rich Gulf region, with its vulnerably weak states and its local conflicts, has aroused fears in the west, particularly after the Soviet occupation of Afghanistan in 1979. Russia has built new air bases disturbingly close to the Mormuz Strait, through which all tankers carrying oil from the Gulf must pass (*46, 49*). The 1970s had already seen the withdrawal of British forces from the Gulf region, and the upheaval in Iran that ended its role as a western-equipped buffer against possible Soviet southward thrusts (*41, 47*).

41 Suez and Indian Ocean

The Suez Canal was built in the 1860s by a French-based international company, by agreement with the rulers of Turkey and Egypt. In 1882 the British occupied Egypt, thus completing a strategic chain in which the main links were Gibraltar, Malta, Suez and Aden. The Suez route became Britain's main imperial 'life-line' to its possessions in the east – which at one time included India, Burma, Malaya, Australia, New Zealand, much of East Africa, and many islands in the Indian Ocean and the Pacific. The protection of this life-line was a British preoccupation. Moreover, Britain later became dependent for three-quarters of its oil supplies on tankers from the Middle East passing through the Suez Canal (40).

When Egypt became independent in 1922 Britain retained control of its defence; under the 1936 treaty British forces withdrew from most of Egypt but remained in the Canal zone; in the 1939–45 war, when British and Commonwealth forces repelled German and Italian attempts to capture the Canal and reach the Indian Ocean, the Canal zone became a major British base. This base was finally evacuated, on Egyptian insistence, a few months before the 1956 Suez conflict (42).

Meanwhile the British relinquishment of empire had begun with the granting of independence to India and Pakistan in 1947. The process had almost been completed, 'east of Suez', by 1967 – when, as a result of the 'Six-Day War' (42), the Canal was closed until 1975. In 1968 Britain announced plans to remove its remaining forces from Singapore and the small Gulf states (46, 62) by 1971. Among the Indian Ocean islands, Britain gave independence to the Maldives in 1965 (although they did not become a Commonwealth member until 1982), to Mauritius in 1968 and to Seychelles in 1976 (when the islands of Aldabra, Desroches and Farquhar were transferred to Seychelles control).

With the age of British predominance in the Indian Ocean thus ended, the Suez Canal lost much of its former strategic importance. However, the new situation in the region carried an echo of the 19th-century period when the British saw Russia's conquest of Central Asia (53) as a threat to their Indian empire and feared that it would try to reach the Indian Ocean by way of Iran. Tsarist Russia had been deterred from occupying

Afghanistan, but the USSR was not (*49*). And the USSR, which had built up a powerful navy, was now able to maintain a naval force in the Indian Ocean, using the bases it had acquired on the coasts of Vietnam, Ethiopia, and South Yemen, whose communist-led regime also controlled Socotra island (*35, 45, 60*).

The former Soviet bases in Somalia were now, however, available to the Americans, who were also maintaining a naval presence in the region and negotiating about facilities in Oman, where Britain had withdrawn in 1977 from its former base on Masira island (*35, 46*). Farther south, the Americans were building base facilities on Diego Garcia island, in the Chagos group – officially, since 1965, the British Indian Ocean Territory (BIOT). This last remaining British dependency in the region had presented its own problems. In 1982 Britain agreed to pay compensation to the former plantation workers who had been moved from Diego Garcia to Mauritius between 1965 and 1973; meanwhile Mauritius put in a claim to the Chagos group.

Reunion remained an overseas *département* of France, which also had base facilities at Djibouti (*35*). France had granted independence to Madagascar in 1960 and to the Comoros in 1975; but the people of Mayotte, one of the Comoro islands, had insisted on retaining French protection; and Madagascar laid claims to several uninhabited islands on which France maintained weather stations (one of them, Tromelin, was also claimed by Mauritius).

The Seychelles regime installed by a coup in 1977 survived two attempted counter-coups in 1981 and 1982. The 1981 one had involved mercenaries recruited in, and flown in from, South Africa. The regime called in troops from Tanzania to its aid.

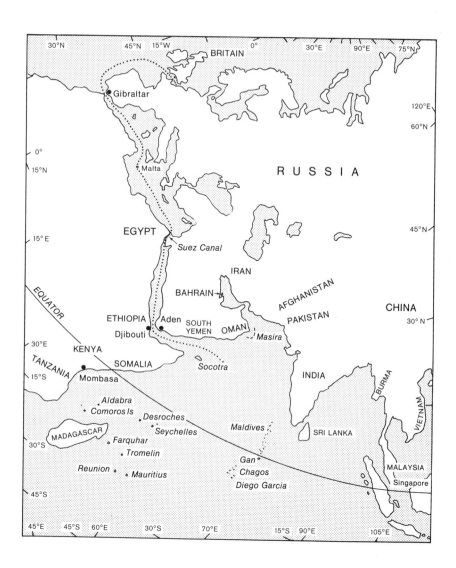

42 Israel and Arabs – I

The area shown in these maps was formerly all within the Turkish empire. After the 1914–18 war, under League of Nations mandates, Syria and Lebanon were taken over by France; Palestine and Transjordan, by Britain. The Palestine mandate provided for the creation of a Jewish 'national home', without damage to the existing population's interests – a difficult aim. Since the 1890s the Zionist movement had been promoting Jewish settlement in Palestine, but in 1920 there were only about 60,000 Jews there, and 600,000 Arabs. Under the mandate Jewish immigration increased, especially when the persecution of Jews began in Nazi Germany (*18*); and Arab–Jewish hostility boiled up. After the Nazis' massacre of millions of Jews during the 1939–45 war Zionism won wider support, particularly in America; survivors of the 'Holocaust' struggled to reach Palestine; the British found it very hard to restrict Jewish entry and curb the mounting Arab–Jewish conflicts. In 1947 Britain announced that it would withdraw from Palestine and put the problem before the United Nations. By then there were about 600,000 Jews, 1,100,000 Moslem Arabs and 150,000 (mainly Arab) Christians in Palestine.

The UN Assembly approved a plan (backed by both the US and the USSR) to partition Palestine, with Jerusalem, which would have fallen within the Arab state, internationalized. The Arabs rejected the plan. In 1948 the British pulled out. The Jews proclaimed the new state of Israel, but it was at once attacked by all the neighbouring Arab countries, while fighting also continued between Palestinian Arabs and Jews.

When UN mediation secured armistices in 1949, the Israelis were left holding more territory than the partition plan had assigned to them, including part of Jerusalem. Transjordan – an independent state since 1946 – annexed the other half of Jerusalem and the hilly regions of Samaria and Judaea (the 'West Bank') and renamed itself the Kingdom of Jordan. Egypt held the 'Gaza Strip'. Most of the former Arab inhabitants of what was now Israel had become refugees, surviving with UN aid, in Gaza, Jordan and other Arab states. The Arab governments refused to make peace, or recognize Israel, or let its ships use the Suez Canal or the Gulf of Aqaba to reach the Indian Ocean (*41*). Despite the efforts of UN truce observers, Arab raids and Israeli retaliations recurred.

1946

Latakia
Hama
Homs
LEBANON
BEIRUT
Damascus
SYRIA
Haifa
PALESTINE
Jordan
Tel Aviv
Amman
JERUSALEM
Gaza
Dead Sea
TRANSJORDAN
EGYPT
Aqaba

0 miles 50
0 km 50

1950

BEIRUT
LEBANON
Haifa
Nablus
JORDAN
Tel Aviv
Jaffa
Jericho
JERUSALEM
Hebron
Gaza
Beersheba
Dimona
ISRAEL
Negev Desert
EGYPT
Eilat
Aqaba

0 miles 50
0 km 50

In 1956 tension increased on the Israel–Egypt border. Meanwhile an international crisis developed when Egypt expropriated the Suez Canal Company and rebuffed the major canal-using countries' proposals for a new international regime for the Canal (*6, 41*). In October Israel attacked and defeated the Egyptian army in Sinai. When Israel's troops got close to the Suez Canal, the British and French governments demanded to be allowed to take control of it; they claimed that their aim was merely to protect the Canal, but in fact they also wanted to strike a blow at Egypt, which was then contesting their influence throughout the Arab world; the extent of their collusion with Israel was fully revealed later. Egypt rejected their demands. British bombing destroyed much of Egypt's air force on the ground. British and French troops captured Port Said and moved south along the Canal. The UN Assembly called for British, French and Israeli withdrawals and approved the sending of a UN Emergency Force (UNEF) to speed the withdrawals and help avert further conflict. By January 1957 the British and French had left Egypt, and Israel was occupying only Gaza and Sharm el Sheikh at the Gulf of Aqaba's mouth; it withdrew from these areas in March. By April the UN had cleared the Canal, which Egypt had blocked by sinking ships in it.

Egypt continued to bar Israeli ships from the Canal, but they were now able to use the Gulf of Aqaba, where a UNEF unit was posted at Sharm el Sheikh. UNEF successfully policed Israel's border with Egypt from 1957 to 1967, but raids and reprisals continued on the borders with Syria and Jordan.

In 1967 there was particular tension on the Syrian border. In May Egypt moved a large army up to the Israel border, demanded UNEF's immediate removal, and reoccupied Sharm el Sheikh, announcing a new blockade in the Gulf of Aqaba. Israel's appeals to the UN brought it no reassurance, and in June it attacked Egypt, Syria and Jordan. In this 'Six-Day War' Israel captured the whole West Bank; Gaza and all of Sinai right up to the Suez Canal; and the Golan heights, from which Syria had been able to bombard the Galilee lowlands. A new wave of Arab refugees went east across the Jordan river.

The Suez Canal was now an unusable 'front line', but Israel could still use the Gulf of Aqaba. Israel had acquired better defence lines; but it had also acquired territories – the West Bank and Gaza – that had large Arab populations. With all of Palestine now in Israeli hands, the Palestine Arabs seemed to develop a stronger spirit of resistance. Rival guerrilla groups combined in the Palestine Liberation Organization (PLO) – although the rivalries remained, different Arab states backed different

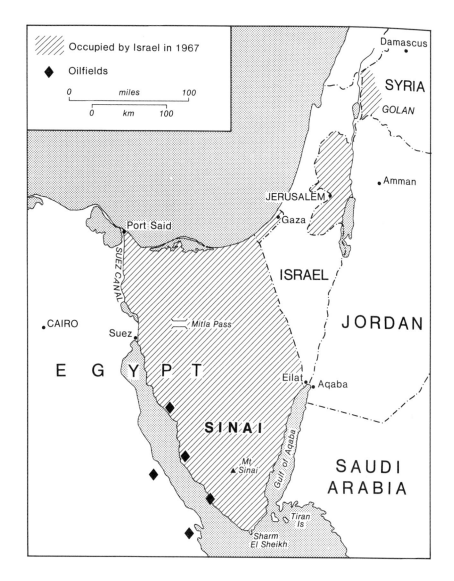

Map legend:
- Occupied by Israel in 1967
- ◆ Oilfields

0   miles   100

0   km   100

Damascus

SYRIA

GOLAN

•Amman

JERUSALEM

Gaza

Port Said

SUEZ CANAL

ISRAEL

•CAIRO

Suez

Mitla Pass

JORDAN

E G Y P T

Eilat

•Aqaba

S I N A I

Mt
▲Sinai

Gulf of Aqaba

SAUDI
ARABIA

Tiran
Is

Sharm
El Sheikh

groups, and terrorist actions in western countries conflicted with the PLO's bids to win international support. In 1970–71 the Palestinian guerrillas in Jordan challenged its government's authority, were defeated by its army, and lost their bases there. As a result the PLO became mainly based in Lebanon (*44*).

43 Israel and Arabs – II

In 1973 Egypt and Syria launched simultaneous attacks on the Sinai and Golan fronts on 6 October (when Israelis were performing the religious ceremonies of Yom Kippur). The Syrians, after capturing Kuneitra, were quickly driven back and the Israelis advanced to within 25 miles of Damascus. The Egyptians crossed the Suez Canal at five points and began to advance eastwards; but by 24 October, when the fighting in Sinai stopped, an Israeli force had crossed the canal near Ismailia, turned south and encircled the town of Suez, cutting off the Egyptian forces east of the southern part of the Canal. The 'Yom Kippur war' greatly heightened international tensions. During the fighting Russia sent arms to the Arab belligerents, America sent arms to Israel, and there was fear of a more direct confrontation between the two superpowers; and Arab governments cut oil supplies to western countries. This resort to the 'oil weapon' set off the first wave of steep oil price rises that severely affected the world economy (*3*).

The UN obtained cease-fires, sent a second UNEF (*42*) to Sinai and, after renewed fighting on the Golan front early in 1974, also provided a small 'disengagement observer force' (UNDOF) to man a narrow buffer zone there between the Syrian and Israeli armies. On that front, the Israelis withdrew a little to the west of the line they had held since 1967, leaving Kuneitra in the zone policed by UNDOF. In Sinai, a series of Israeli withdrawals in 1974–76 released the trapped Egyptian army and allowed Egypt to occupy the whole east bank of the Suez Canal (which was reopened in 1975), with UNEF manning a buffer zone that ran from the Mediterranean to the Gulf of Suez. The United States had played a very active part in bringing about this disengagement of forces, and American diplomacy's full resources were now committed to a sustained effort to avert a further conflict between Israel and its Arab neighbours – particularly Egypt. As one contribution to this, a sophisticated early warning system manned by American civilians was installed in Sinai to support UNEF's buffer role.

Egypt's relations with the USSR, which had long been its main supplier of arms, were worsened by Russia's support for Libya in its quarrels with Egypt (*38*), by Russia's interventions in Ethiopia (*35*) and

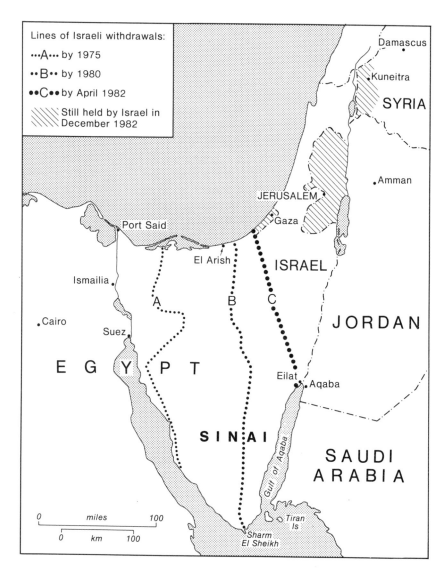

Lines of Israeli withdrawals:
···A··· by 1975
··B·· by 1980
··C·· by April 1982
///// Still held by Israel in
///// December 1982

Damascus
Kuneitra
SYRIA
Amman
JERUSALEM
Gaza
Port Said
El Arish
ISRAEL
Ismailia
A   B   C
Cairo
Suez
JORDAN
E G Y P T
Eilat
Aqaba
S I N A I
Gulf of Aqaba
SAUDI
ARABIA
0   miles   100
0   km   100
Tiran Is
Sharm El Sheikh

by other Soviet actions; increasingly, Egypt sought and obtained
American help. In 1977 President Anwar Sadat startled the world by
visiting Israel and starting a series of high-level Egyptian–Israeli talks.
His peace initiative was nearly scuppered by Israel's invasion of Lebanon
in 1978 (*44*); but, later in that year, the Egyptian and Israeli leaders met as

115

President Carter's guests at Camp David, his rural retreat north-west of Washington, DC. These talks produced outline agreements for both an Egyptian–Israeli settlement and a wider Arab–Israeli one. In 1979 Egypt and Israel signed a peace treaty based on the Camp David agreements. Israel began a new series of withdrawals, which ended in April 1982 with the removal of the last of its forces in Sinai and of the Israeli settlements that had been built there.

The Arab League (29) suspended Egypt from membership, and Russia, wishing to please the Arab governments that condemned Egypt for making peace, blocked the renewal of UNEF's mandate in 1979. However, the Americans found enough support to produce a replacement for UNEF – the 'multinational force and observers' (MFO) which was installed in 1982 in a demilitarized buffer zone in western Sinai running along the Egypt–Israel border and southwards to Sharm el Sheikh. Israel now had freedom of movement through both the Gulf of Aqaba and the Suez Canal.

In 1980 Israel's parliament adopted a law declaring Jerusalem to be Israel's 'united capital'. In 1981 Israel virtually annexed the occupied Golan area by enacting that its laws should apply there. In June 1982 it launched its second large-scale invasion of Lebanon (44). Its peace treaty with Egypt survived the angry reactions to these successive moves, but progress towards a fuller normalizing of the two countries' relations was checked. Throughout, there remained the underlying problem of the occupied West Bank and Gaza. The peace treaty had provided that negotiations should be held with the aim of giving these areas autonomy. The negotiations became deadlocked within a year. It became increasingly clear that the Israeli government's idea of autonomy for the occupied areas was a very limited one, and unacceptable to Egypt as well as to the Palestinians. Meanwhile Israel had speeded up the creation of Jewish settlements all over the West Bank. By 1982 about two-fifths of all the land in the West Bank had passed into Israeli hands by one means or another; over 100 settlements had been built, 25,000 Jews were already settled in them and a target of 100,000 settlers had been set for 1985. (These figures exclude East Jerusalem.)

Hopes that the PLO (42) might recognize Israel and acknowledge its right to exist within secure frontiers, and hopes that Israel might agree that the PLO should be brought into negotiations for a peaceful settlement, had been repeatedly raised, but then always deflated, up to 1982. By then the number of Jews in Israel was over three million; there were also about 600,000 non-Jews, mostly Arabs, within Israel's pre-

Occupied territories

Jewish settlements in West Bank (1982)

HAIFA

Mount Carmel

Galilee

Tiberias
Nazareth

Golan

SYRIA

Megiddo

Irbid

Sharon

Samaria

Netanya

Plain of

Nablus

JORDAN

Jordan

Salt

TEL AVIV-JAFFA

Lod
Rehoboth

Ramallah

Jericho

Amman

Ashdod

JERUSALEM

Ashqelon

Bethlehem

I S R A E L

Dead Sea

Gaza

Hebron

Beersheba

| 0 | miles | 20 |
| 0 | km | 20 |

1967 borders, and about $1\frac{1}{4}$ million in the West Bank and Gaza Strip. Outside Palestine, the dispersed Palestine Arabs were estimated to number about $1\frac{1}{4}$ million in Jordan, $\frac{3}{4}$ million in Lebanon and Syria, and nearly a million elsewhere (a majority of these being in the Gulf oilfield regions – 46).

44 Lebanon

Alone among Arab states Lebanon is half Christian, half Moslem. Under Turkish rule it was given a special status; under the French mandate it was separated from Syria (45). Constitutional compromises were devised, but these gave the Christians advantages which the Moslems came to resent, while the Christians came to fear submergence in the surrounding Moslem Arab world. When Syria joined Egypt in the UAR in 1958 tension rose; Lebanon, seeking reassurance, obtained a UN observer group and then, for a few months, an American force (45). That crisis died down. But after 1970 the Palestine Liberation Organization (PLO), having been forced out of Jordan, concentrated its guerrilla forces in Lebanon, where there had been large communities of Palestinian refugees since 1948 (42). The guerrillas' attacks on Israel brought reprisals; eventually Lebanon cracked under the strain.

In 1975 civil war broke out. In this confused struggle, the main conflicts were between the Palestinians, with their leftist Lebanese allies, and the Kataeb militia formed by the Maronites (the biggest Christian sect, named from the 5th-century St Maro). Each side destroyed the other's isolated strongholds; a sort of partition took shape, the Christians holding a zone running north from Beirut, while the PLO and its allies dominated the south and also held Tripoli and areas near the northern frontier. The capital, Beirut, became a battlefield. In 1976 Syria sent in troops. The Syrians occupied Tripoli and the Bekaa valley and advanced to Beirut. Their intervention stopped the civil war and at first helped the hard-pressed Christians, but by late 1978 the Syrians' shelling of Christian-held East Beirut was causing international tension; meanwhile many Moslem Lebanese became suspicious about the Syrians' motives as their occupation looked like becoming a permanent one.

In March 1978 Israel, aiming to stop PLO raiding and rocket fire across its northern border, occupied Lebanon south of the Litani river (except Tyre, where the PLO held out). A UN force was sent to replace the Israelis as they withdrew and to restore Lebanese authority in the south; but when the Israelis withdrew in June they handed over control of a zone along the border not to the UN force but to a local militia headed by Major Haddad, which had been holding a Christian enclave around

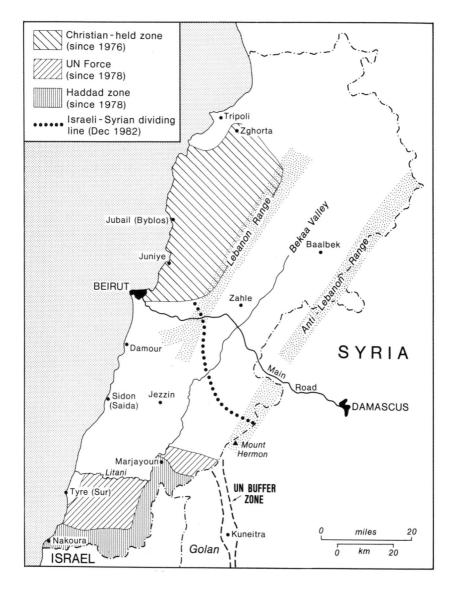

Legend:
- Christian-held zone (since 1976)
- UN Force (since 1978)
- Haddad zone (since 1978)
- Israeli-Syrian dividing line (Dec 1982)

Tripoli
Zghorta
Jubail (Byblos)
Juniye
Lebanon Range
Bekaa Valley
Baalbek
Anti-Lebanon Range
BEIRUT
Zahle
Damour
SYRIA
Main Road
Sidon (Saida)
Jezzin
DAMASCUS
Mount Hermon
Marjayoun
Litani
Tyre (Sur)
UN BUFFER ZONE
Nakoura
Kuneitra
Golan
ISRAEL

0 miles 20
0 km 20

Marjayoun. The UN force could not even create a continuous buffer zone, and in the two areas that it occupied it was repeatedly attacked by Haddad's Israeli-supplied militia as well as by the PLO. (In contrast, UNDOF, the neighbouring UN force in Syria's Golan region, was

119

able to patrol its narrow buffer zone without harassment from either side – *43*).

In 1981, when the Syrians besieged Zahle, a Christian-held town, and moved anti-aircraft missiles into the Bekaa valley, fears arose of open war between Syria and Israel, which by then seemed to be committed to supporting the Kataeb. American diplomacy eased this crisis, like others, but tension remained high and it was widely predicted that Israel would soon invade Lebanon again.

In June 1982 it did so. This time Israeli forces moved swiftly up the coast as far as Beirut, linked up with the Kataeb there and even sent units into the Christian-held zone to the north, while other Israeli units took over all the formerly PLO-held area in southern Lebanon. About 11,000 PLO guerrillas were trapped in West Beirut. After several weeks of Israeli siege and bombardment, and hectic American and Arab diplomacy, it was agreed in August that they should be evacuated – a majority of them going to Syria, the rest to seven other Arab states. The PLO thus lost both its Beirut headquarters and its hold on southern Lebanon; but PLO forces remained in the Syrian-held zone in the north, and many thousands of Palestinian refugees remained in both north and south Lebanon. Under Israel's protection, the Kataeb militia began to extend its control southwards (and soon clashed with the Druzes – a distinctive community that broke away from Islam 900 years ago – in the hills south-east of Beirut). Israeli and Syrian forces faced each other along a line running north-west from Mount Hermon. A joint American, French and Italian peacekeeping force was temporarily placed in Beirut. (Israel would not agree to a UN force being placed there; its government had come to regard the UN as hostile.)

45 Arabia

Arabia – the Arabian peninsula and the Arab lands north of it – was formerly dominated by Turkey. Turkish rule waned, was ended by the 1914–18 war, and was followed by a period of British and French control of much of the region; but Saudi Arabia and Yemen emerged as independent states.

The Kingdom of Saudi Arabia had taken its present shape by 1933. From a base among the Wahabi (puritan) Arabs of the Nejd, the Saud family had extended its power over the Hasa, Hejaz and Asir regions. Oil production, from 1939 on, turned a formerly poor, largely desert, country into the world's biggest oil exporter (40). The oil revenues gave Saudi Arabia much influence; it financed other states when they were in difficulties – notably Egypt, and more recently Iraq (48); once the big oil price rises began (3), the disposition of its funds, and its decisions on pricing and output, affected world economic trends. It remained a very conservative and religious country – the guardian of Islam's holiest place, Mecca (28).

Yemen is mountainous but relatively fertile and populous. During its 1962–69 civil war Saudi Arabia financed one side and Egypt sent 50,000 soldiers to fight for the other. Egypt withdrew its army after its defeat by Israel in 1967 (42), but Russia then poured in arms and thus prevented the Saudi-backed forces from capturing the capital, Sana. The fighting died down, and a period of uneasy compromises, disturbed by new revolts, coups and assassinations, followed.

South Yemen became independent in 1967. Britain had held Aden since 1839 and had made treaties with local rulers, eventually turning its protectorate into the Federation of South Arabia. When it became clear that the British were leaving, a struggle developed between rival forces. The conservative groups, and one backed by Egypt, were defeated by a far-left one which, taking power when the British left in 1967, became dependent on Soviet support. As a port, Aden did not recover after the 1967–75 closing of the Suez Canal; but Russia acquired valuable naval facilities at Aden and on the islands of Perim, in the Bab el Mandeb strait, and Socotra (41).

Oman (formerly Muscat and Oman), after a period of British protection, asserted its full independence in 1970. Britain used a base on

Masira island until 1977, and helped Oman to suppress revolts in the Dhofar area which South Yemen fostered. By 1982 Dhofar was quiet and South Yemen seemed to want better relations with Oman.

In 1981 the Gulf Co-operation Council (GCC) was formed by Saudi Arabia, Oman and the small Gulf states, Kuwait, Bahrain, Qatar and the United Arab Emirates (46), partly because of growing concern about regional defence. This concern deepened as the Iran–Iraq war went on; Iraq became dependent on subsidies from the oil-rich GCC states; and Iran, resenting their support for Iraq, gave them ominous warnings and worked on their Shia inhabitants' feelings (28, 48).

In the north, after 1918, Syria and Lebanon came under French rule, Iraq, Palestine and Transjordan under British rule, until the 1940s (42, 44). In 1958 a military regime replaced Iraq's former pro-western government, which, in the 1955 Baghdad Pact, had joined with Britain, Iran, Pakistan and Turkey in an American-backed 'northern tier' alliance intended to form a barrier between Russia and the Middle East. Iraq withdrew from the alliance – which was reshaped in 1959 as the Central Treaty Organization (CENTO), worked mainly on economic co-operation, and petered out with the withdrawal of Iran and Pakistan in 1979. Iraq developed links with Russia, but it was disenchanted by Russia's failure to support it in the Iran–Iraq war.

Syria and Egypt formed the United Arab Republic (UAR) in 1958 (29). This move, and Iraq's 1958 change of regime, caused alarm in Lebanon, which complained of UAR support for Lebanese rebels, and Jordan. They sought help from the USA, which sent troops to Lebanon, and from Britain, which sent troops to Jordan; both these forces withdrew three months later, when inter-Arab relations had become less tense. Syria, having come to resent Egyptian domination, withdrew from the UAR in 1961. Thereafter, a succession of military regimes ruled Syria, sometimes with great brutality; after a rising in Hama (42) in February 1982 the army destroyed much of the city, killing 20,000 people. Since 1976 the Syrian army has occupied a large part of Lebanon (44).

The Kurds, a Moslem people of about 18 millions, whose language is distantly related to Persian, inhabit a large area in Iran, Iraq, Syria, Turkey and the Soviet borderland. In Iraq, whose northern oilfields lie in the Kurdish region, the Kurds have at times forced governments to promise them some autonomy; elsewhere, they have obtained none. In 1982 Iran and Iraq, as well as fighting each other, both faced continuing Kurdish rebellions.

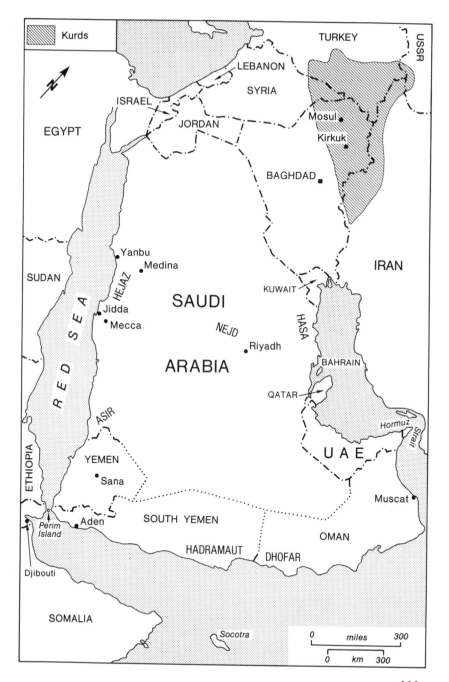

Kurds

TURKEY

USSR

LEBANON

SYRIA

ISRAEL

JORDAN

Mosul

Kirkuk

EGYPT

BAGHDAD

IRAN

Yanbu

Medina

SUDAN

HEJAZ

SAUDI

KUWAIT

HASA

RED SEA

Jidda

Mecca

NEJD

Riyadh

BAHRAIN

ARABIA

QATAR

Hormuz

ASIR

UAE

Straits

ETHIOPIA

YEMEN

Sana

Muscat

Perim
Island

Aden

SOUTH YEMEN

OMAN

Djibouti

HADRAMAUT

DHOFAR

SOMALIA

Socotra

0   miles   300

0   km   300

46 Gulf states

Kuwait, Bahrain, Qatar and the seven little states that were once called Trucial Oman – Abu Dhabi, Dubai, Sharjah, Ajman, Umm al Qaiwain, Ras al Khaimah and Fujairah – were all formerly under British protection by treaty. Kuwait became fully independent in 1961, Bahrain and Qatar in 1971; six of the Trucial states formed the independent United Arab Emirates (UAE) in 1971, and Ras al Khaimah joined them in 1972. When Kuwait became independent, Iraq threatened to annex it; a small British force was sent to protect it, but soon replaced by a joint Arab League force; Iraq abandoned its claim in 1963. Iran, which had long maintained a claim to Bahrain, renounced it in 1970; but in 1971 Iran occupied the two small Tumbs islands and Abu Musa, which were claimed by UAE member states.

In 1981 all the small Gulf states joined with Saudi Arabia and Oman in forming the Gulf Co-operation Council (45). All the six GCC members have oilfields (some of them offshore) and have been enriched by the past decade's big oil price rises (3). Kuwait's oil wealth is outstanding; in the 1960s it was producing more oil than Saudi Arabia. In the UAE, oil output has hitherto been concentrated in Abu Dhabi and secondarily in Dubai. With the oil boom, the UAE's population has swollen to over a million, more than half of it drawn from India, Pakistan and Bangladesh; Palestinian Arabs are also numerous among the immigrants in the UAE and other oilfield states. There are old-established Iranian communities along the Arab side of the Gulf, and larger communities of Arabs of the Shia sect of Islam. The region's dominant Sunnis have become more apprehensive about the influence of 'revolutionary' and Shia Iran since the outbreak of the Iran–Iraq war (28, 47, 48).

All the small Gulf states' oil is shipped out through the Hormuz (Ormuz) Strait; fortunately for them, both sides in the Iran–Iraq war (which has often been called 'the Gulf war') seemed to recognize an interest in keeping the strait open. The name of the Gulf itself has become a bone of contention: once it was usually called the Persian Gulf; Arab pressure for it to be called the Arabian Gulf has led to the common practice of calling it simply the Gulf. (But in oilmen's jargon the word 'Gulf' may still refer to the Gulf of Mexico.)

U A E - United Arab Emirates

IRAQ

Bandar Khomeini

0   *miles*   200

0   *km*   200

KUWAIT

Kharg Island

IRAN

Ras Tannurah

Damman   BAHRAIN
Dhahran

Abu Musa
and Tumbs Is

to
Oman

QATAR

Doha

Umm al Qaiwain

Ras al Khaimah

Sharjah   Ajman

Dubai   Fujairah

SAUDI ARABIA

Abu Dhabi

U   A   E

OMAN

125

47 Iran

In Iran (known as Persia before 1935) only half of the 40 million people are Farsi-speaking Persians. A third are Azerbaijani Turks; near the western frontier there are Kurdish and Arab minorities, near the eastern one Turkmens and Baluchs (45, 48, 49). Population is concentrated in the north-west; a large region stretching east from near the capital, Teheran, is almost empty desert.

During the 1939–45 war British and Soviet forces occupied Iran, and the western allies sent vital supplies to Russia across it. In 1945 the Russians, angry because Iran would not grant them oilfield concessions, held on to the north-western regions and set up puppet Azerbaijani and Kurdish governments there. Western pressure made them withdraw in 1946, but Iranian fear of Russia had been heightened. Although postwar Iran asserted itself against western economic power, expropriating the British oil company in 1951 (40), it joined the western-backed Baghdad Pact in 1955 (45) and later, especially after the withdrawal of British forces from the Gulf states in 1971 (41, 46), it greatly increased its military strength, with aid and encouragement from the United States – which hoped that Iran would be a barrier against the Soviet encroachment into the Middle East indicated by Russia's arms supplies to Iraq and Syria.

In the 1970s the regime headed by the Shah met mounting internal opposition. The Shah's enthusiasm for economic development, education and social reforms angered Moslem mullahs; his reliance on American help angered leftists. Religious and revolutionary forces, both able to foment mob violence, formed an effective alliance. By the end of 1978 Iran was in turmoil – and its oil exports had been halted, setting off the second big wave of worldwide oil price rises (3). In 1979 the Shah was forced into exile and power passed into the hands of fanatical Islamic fundamentalists, headed by Ayatollah Khomeini (28). Religious persecution and arbitrary executions on a massive scale soon made the new regime appear far more oppressive than the Shah's.

In November 1979 the American embassy in Teheran was seized and its staff were held as hostages. The USA pressed for sanctions against Iran and, in April 1980, unsuccessfully tried to rescue the hostages; but

they were not set free until January 1981. Meanwhile Iran's self-imposed isolation had encouraged Iraq to invade it (*48*).

Iran denounced Russia's invasion of Afghanistan (*49*), which impeded Soviet attempts to exploit the new Iranian rulers' bitter anti-Americanism. Afghan refugees fled into Iran as well as into Pakistan. By 1982 the Iraqi invaders had been pushed back to the frontier; but the Iranian forces had not been able to subdue the Kurdish rebellion near that frontier (*45*). The regime in Teheran still looked unstable. There were fears that, if it collapsed, the Russians might move in as they had done in Afghanistan, or that, if it survived, its need for external conflicts as diversions might lead it to turn upon the small Gulf states (*46*).

48 Iran and Iraq

The war that broke out in September 1980 between Iran and Iraq followed a long period of disputes between them, particularly over control of the Shatt al Arab, the waterway through which the Euphrates and Tigris rivers flow into the Gulf, and on which stand Basra, Iraq's main port, and Iran's port of Khorramshahr and Abadan oil refineries. Iraq encouraged separatism among the Arab inhabitants of Khuzestan, Iran's south-western province. Iran urged the Shia Arabs in southern Iraq to shake off their Sunni rulers (28). After many minor clashes on the border, Iraq started a full-scale war in the belief that Iran, internationally isolated by its own actions, with its affairs in chaos and its army demoralized after the ousting of the Shah (47), could show little resistance. This belief proved to be unfounded.

The Iraqi forces seized large areas along the border but captured no large cities except Khorramshahr (which was devastated by the long struggle there). They besieged Abadan but failed to take it. The war became an alternation of fierce battles and long periods of stalemate. By 1982 the Iraqis had been pushed back to the frontier at almost every point along the line, and the Iranians had retaken the ruins of Khorramshahr and crossed the frontier in the south, threatening Basra. Iraq was asking for peace, but Iran seemed in no mood to make terms that Iraq could accept.

Throughout the war, Iraq's trade through Basra and its oil shipments through the Gulf were blocked. It exported some oil through the pipeline running from its northern fields across Turkey, but it became heavily dependent on subsidies from Saudi Arabia and the small Gulf oil states, and on overland supply routes through Jordan and Kuwait. (Syria, instead of siding with its Arab neighbour, had openly backed Iran.) In contrast, Iran's main oil terminal on Kharg island had continued to operate. (Iraqi attacks on Kharg in late 1982 were reported to have failed.)

Area seized, then lost by Iraq (1980-1982)

Mahabad

Mosul

K U R D-I-S.T. A N

Kirkuk

Sanandaj

TEHERAN ■

Tigris

Khanaqin

Kermanshah

Qom

Mandali

I R A N

BAGHDAD

Mehran

Z A G R O S

Karbala

Kut

Dezful

Esfahan

Amara

Susangerd

M O U N T A I N S

KHUZESTAN

Euphrates

Ahwaz

Basra

Abadan

IRAQ   Khorramshahr

Shatt al Arab

KUWAIT

Fao

Kuwait

Kharg

0   miles   100

0   km   100

SAUDI ARABIA

49 Afghanistan

Russia's invasion of Afghanistan in 1979 affected the whole international climate. Most 'third-world' states, as well as western ones, condemned the invasion and demanded a Soviet withdrawal. In strategic terms, the Russians' occupation of Afghanistan brought them disturbingly close to the Indian Ocean, and particularly close to the Hormuz Strait at the mouth of the Gulf (40, 41).

Afghanistan's 15 million people include about 8 million Pathans and Baluchs, whose kindred live in Pakistan; and 5 million Tajiks, Uzbeks and Turkmens, who are similarly related to the inhabitants of the adjacent territories to the north, which Russia conquered in the 19th century (53). After 1947 (50), the Pathan-dominated government in Kabul pressed for Pakistan's North-West Frontier Province to be made a separate new state, 'Pushtunistan' (Pushtu is the Pathans' language). This led to border conflicts, the disruption of Afghan trade with and through Pakistan, and an increase of Soviet influence in Afghanistan. The Russians built roads and airfields there, whose military value later became clear; and they exploited the big gas field near Shibarghan (whose output now goes to Russia).

Military coups in 1973 and 1978 put a fairly pliant pro-Russian regime in power in Kabul, but resistance grew and the Soviet officers who had been attached to the Afghan army learnt that they could not rely on it. In December 1979 Soviet troops were rushed to Kabul and other key points; Afghanistan's president was killed and a more docile successor installed; but the Afghans did not accept the occupation tamely. A long war began, and the disintegration of the Kabul regime's army (many conscripts went over to join the guerrillas) left the 100,000-strong Soviet forces to do more fighting than they had bargained for. The Russians' greatly superior firepower destroyed many villages and devastated large areas, but failed to crush the guerrilla forces which were formed not only in Pathan areas but also among the Tajiks, Nuristanis, Hazaras and Baluchs. By 1982 about 200,000 Afghans had been killed and over 3 million had fled into Pakistan and Iran; but the war went on, and the Russians could not even keep the larger towns safe from guerrilla attacks.

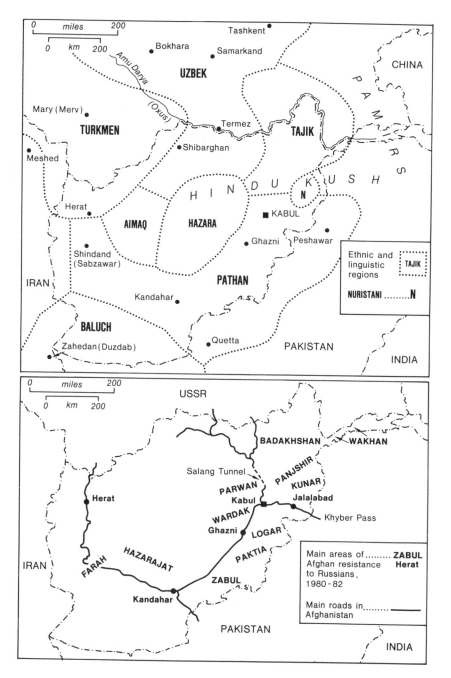

Top map:

0 miles 200
0 km 200

Tashkent

Bokhara
Samarkand

Amu Darya (Oxus)

UZBEK

CHINA

P A M I R S

Mary (Merv)

TURKMEN

Termez

TAJIK

Meshed

Shibarghan

H I N D U K U S H
N

Herat

AIMAQ

HAZARA

KABUL

Ghazni

Peshawar

Ethnic and linguistic regions | TAJIK
NURISTANI ....N

Shindand (Sabzawar)

IRAN

PATHAN

Kandahar

BALUCH

Zahedan (Duzdab)

Quetta

PAKISTAN

INDIA

Bottom map:

0 miles 200
0 km 200

USSR

BADAKHSHAN

WAKHAN

Salang Tunnel

PARWAN

PANJSHIR

KUNAR

Herat

Kabul

Jalalabad

Khyber Pass

WARDAK

Ghazni

LOGAR

HAZARAJAT

PAKTIA

FARAH

ZABUL

IRAN

Kandahar

Main areas of .... **ZABUL**
Afghan resistance **Herat**
to Russians,
1980-82

Main roads in ....
Afghanistan

PAKISTAN

INDIA

50 India and Pakistan 1947–64

Britain's Indian empire was the most spectacular feature of the age of west European colonization in Asia and Africa, and it was the British withdrawal from India in 1947 that set off the great wave of 'decoloniz-ation' throughout those regions (*9*, *27*). Until the 1930s proposals for India's advance to independence had been based on the hope that the huge country could remain united. But in the 1940s leaders of the Moslem minority began to campaign for a separate Moslem state, which they named Pakistan, and it became clear that partition was the only way of preventing all-out Hindu–Moslem war after the British left. Even so, before and after the two nations became independent in 1947, there was widespread fighting, especially in Punjab and Bengal, the two provinces which had to be divided as about half of their inhabitants were Moslems. More than half a million people were killed; about 8 million Moslems fled from India into Pakistan and a similar number of Hindus and Sikhs fled in the opposite direction. However, 40 million Moslems remained in India and 10 million Hindus in Pakistan.

Pakistan emerged as a nation consisting of two 'wings' separated by 1000 miles of Indian territory. Each wing contained about half of its total population. Relations between the wings were never easy; Bengalis complained that the government – based at first in Karachi and later in Islamabad – gave undue favour to the western wing, which comprised Sind, Baluchistan, the North-West Frontier Province and the eastern part of Punjab (*51*).

The partition line cut across the irrigation system fed by the Punjab rivers, tributaries of the Indus. India, controlling most of the headwaters, planned to irrigate more land on its side of the new border; Pakistanis feared that this would deprive much of their best farmland of water. In the 1960 Indus Waters Treaty the two nations agreed on a plan, backed by western aid, to build new dams and canals and thus transfer water from the Indus itself to the areas in Pakistan formerly supplied from the eastern tributaries (*51*).

Most of the princely states which had formerly accepted British paramountcy agreed to accede to one or other of the two new sovereign nations. The Moslem ruler of mainly Hindu-peopled Hyderabad sought

independence, but India took over Hyderabad in 1948. The Hindu ruler of mainly Moslem-peopled Kashmir (formally, Jammu and Kashmir) vacillated; a Moslem revolt broke out, and Pathan tribesmen from Pakistan invaded Kashmir. The ruler then asked India for help and offered to accede to it. India sent troops in, but the Moslems still held northern and western Kashmir in 1949, when the UN secured a cease-fire and sent military observers to Kashmir. The dispute continued to embitter relations between India and Pakistan, and eventually led to the 1965 war (*51*). Meanwhile, India came into conflict with China in north-eastern Kashmir (*52*).

France and Portugal held small territories on or near India's coasts during the period of British rule. The French ones were handed over to India in 1951 and 1954, but Portugal would not contemplate a transfer. Indian impatience mounted, and by 1956 nearly all movement between the Portuguese enclaves and India had been blocked. In 1961 Indian forces took over Goa, Diu and Daman, the last vestiges of European rule in the Indian sub-continent.

Sri Lanka (until 1972, Ceylon) had been a separate British colony before becoming independent in 1948. Its relations with India were complicated by the problem of its Tamil minority (about a fifth of its population of 15 million). Some of these Tamils' ancestors came from south India as recently as the 19th century, but 70% of them represent a community that has been settled in the island for over 1000 years, mainly in the north and east. From 1956 on, recurrent conflicts followed moves to impose more use of Sinhala, the language of the island's majority, and other government actions which were resented by the Tamils (300,000 of whom have been 'repatriated' to India, while others have been unable to obtain Sri Lankan citizenship). In 1976 the island's main Tamil party demanded 'liberation'. Concessions were later made on the language question and on local government, but in 1981–82 there was fresh violence, mainly in the north.

51 India and Pakistan 1965–82

The Rann of Kutch, an area of salt marsh south-east of Sind, is mostly submerged every rainy season, but may have oil potential. The border was not fully demarcated here in 1947, and a long dispute culminated in frontier clashes in early 1965; but India and Pakistan then accepted international arbitration (which produced a settlement in 1968).

Also in 1965, moves to integrate Kashmir more fully into India heightened tension. In August, after Pakistani infiltration across the 1949 cease-fire line, Indian troops launched attacks across the line; Pakistan counter-attacked; in September Indian forces invaded Pakistan itself, both in Sind and in Punjab. The UN obtained a cease-fire, and sent more observers to watch over the two armies' withdrawal from all the areas occupied during the war. Meanwhile China had stepped up pressure along its borders with India (52) and Russia had offered to mediate. Indian and Pakistani leaders met at Tashkent (49) and relations improved, but the Kashmir dispute was not resolved.

Mounting Bengali demands for more self-government for East Pakistan met with repressive action by the Pakistani government in Islamabad, and by 1971 a large part of Pakistan's army was fighting Bengali guerrillas, while several million Bengalis had fled into India. India's army then invaded East Pakistan and defeated the Pakistani forces there. A new independent republic, Bangladesh (population now about 90 million) was proclaimed in what had been East Pakistan. Pakistan was thus reduced to what had formerly been its western wing, and although there were now two Moslem states in the sub-continent the new one, Bangladesh, was to some extent a creation of India's.

Even after Pakistan had had to accept Bangladesh's independence as an accomplished fact, friction continued between the two capitals, Islamabad and Dacca (Dhaka), over many issues, including exchanges of population and division of assets. In Bangladesh, the antagonism between pro-Indian and anti-Indian elements was one cause of the turbulence (including two successful military coups and several unsuccessful ones) that marked its first decade of independent existence. Between 1976 and 1982 India and Bangladesh were at odds over: (1) control of the waters of the Ganges and Brahmaputra rivers, whose joint delta covers most of Bangladesh; (2) possession of a newly formed island (New Moore or South Talpatty Island) on the Bengal coast; (3) clashes on the frontier between India's Tripura state and south-eastern Bangladesh – where the Bangladesh army's operations against rebel hill tribes east of Chittagong had caused thousands of refugees to cross into India; (4) large-scale migration from Bangladesh into Assam and Tripura.

In India, meanwhile, a new set of state borders had appeared since 1947. The former princely states were absorbed, and the new states were based mainly on linguistic regions: Kerala, for speakers of Malayalam; Tamil Nadu, for Tamil; Andhra Pradesh, for Telugu; Karnataka (until 1973, Mysore), for Kanarese (Kannada); Orissa, for Oriya; West Bengal, for Bengali; Rajasthan, Uttar Pradesh (formerly United Provinces), Madhya Pradesh and Bihar, for Hindi and its variants. In 1960 two states, Gujarat, for Gujarati-speakers, and Maharashtra, for Marathi, were formed out of the former state of Bombay. In 1966 the part of Punjab left to India by partition was redivided; the mainly Hindi-speaking part became Haryana, the Himalayan foothills areas went to Himachal Pradesh, the residual Punjab being mainly Punjabi-speaking and predominantly Sikh (but many Sikhs were still unsatisfied, and agitation for greater autonomy was continuing among them in 1982).

In the north-east, the state of Assam was diminished by the creation of new states for the peoples of the hill areas around the Brahmaputra valley: in 1962 Nagaland, with its capital at Kohima, for the Nagas; in 1972 Meghalaya, for the peoples of the Garo, Khasi and Jaintia Hills. Two former princely states, Manipur and Tripura, were given full statehood in 1972, when two new 'union territories' were also constituted: Mizoram (formerly the Mizo or Lushai Hills), and Arunachal Pradesh (formerly the North-East Frontier Agency). These changes did not end all of the Naga and Mizo guerrilla activity which had started in the 1950s; and in 1982 there was some similar activity in Manipur.

Other 'union territories' in India include the federal capital, Delhi; the Andaman and Nicobar islands; Lakshadweep (the Laccadive, Minicoy and Amindivi islands); and the former French and Portuguese territories of Pondicherry and Goa (50).

AP	Arunachal Pradesh
HP	Himachal Pradesh
Ma	Manipur
Me	Meghalaya
Mi	Mizoram
N	Nagaland
NWFP	N–W Frontier Province
S	Sikkim
T	Tripura
WB	West Bengal

137

52 Himalayas

Since the 1950s the Himalayan mountain range, formerly regarded as a clear natural dividing line, has become the scene of many disputes and clashes. This has changed Asia's strategic geography. Previously India, so often invaded through the Afghan passes in the north-west, had never faced a serious threat from the north-east.

Tibet, although long under China's formal suzerainty, had been in practice an independent state, loosely ruled by the successive Dalai Lamas who were also the religious leaders of a devoutly Buddhist people. In 1950 its small army could not prevent the occupation of Tibet by the communist forces which in 1949 had been victorious in China's civil war (*54, 55*). Large numbers of Chinese were settled in Tibet, coming to

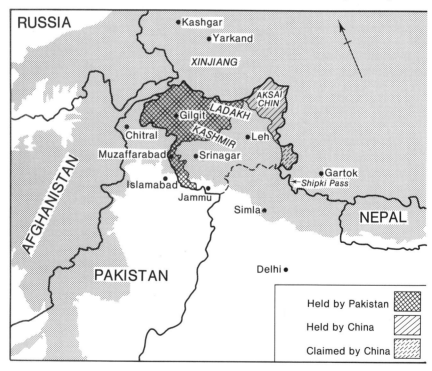

outnumber the Tibetans. Local revolts broke out and were suppressed. In 1959, after riots in Lhasa, the Dalai Lama escaped to India, together with about 12,000 Tibetans.

Meanwhile China had aroused fears in India by publishing maps that showed as Chinese several mountain areas which had long been regarded as belonging to India, Nepal and Bhutan. There were border clashes near the Shipki Pass and elsewhere. In 1958 India protested about China's building of a military road linking Yarkand with Tibet across the Aksai Chin area, in the north-east of Kashmir. China offered to discuss demarcation, but indicated that it meant to hold on to Aksai Chin. In 1959 there was a clash on the border north of Assam, where in 1914, after negotiations with both China and Tibet, the British who then ruled India and Burma had fixed the frontier called the McMahon Line.

In 1960–61 China agreed on frontier lines with Nepal and Burma. It dropped its claim to the Kachin hill area in north Burma, thus accepting the Burmese part of the McMahon Line. In 1962–63 China also negotiated a settlement of its frontier with the Pakistani-held part of

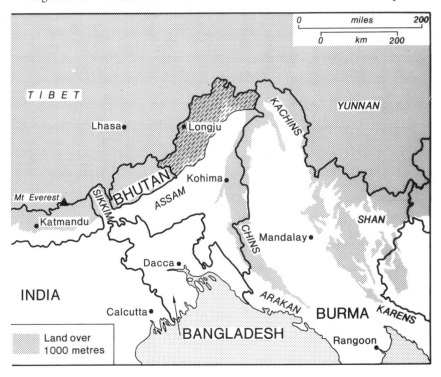

Kashmir (*50*, *51*), despite protests from India – which protested again in 1982 when China and Pakistan opened a new road over the Karakoram range in this sector, linking Kashgar with Gilgit and thence with Islamabad.

The border dispute between China and India worsened in 1961–62, and in October 1962 the Chinese launched a full-scale attack both in Aksai Chin, where they overran India's outposts, and in the north-east, where they advanced almost to the edge of the Assam plains. In December China pulled back its forces in the north-east (which it had difficulty in supplying across the Himalayas) to the McMahon Line; but it kept its grip on Aksai Chin, and maintained its claims in the north-east.

During the 1965 India–Pakistan war (*51*) China accused India of violating its border near Sikkim and demanded an immediate withdrawal. India denied the charge, no armed clash occurred, and when the war ended no more was heard of China's accusation, which had clearly been meant to show support for Pakistan. China maintained that support after the 1971 India–Pakistan war, notably by blocking the admission of Bangladesh to the UN until 1974. Later, relations between China and India improved; but in 1982 China was still maintaining its claims in the area north of Assam, and India remained suspicious about Chinese support for secessionist movements in north-eastern India (*51*).

Bhutan, although an independent kingdom, had for many years a treaty with Britain, which handled its foreign relations; in 1949 it made a similar treaty with India. In 1971 it asserted its separate identity by joining the UN. Sikkim, in whose affairs the British and, after 1947, the Indians had been more directly involved, came under effective Indian control in 1973 and became India's 22nd federal state in 1975, when Sikkim's monarchy was abolished.

Nepal had long guarded its independence carefully; two centuries ago it fought wars against both the Chinese in Tibet and the British in India. Indian influence in Katmandu increased in the 1950s but was later reduced again as Nepal slowly developed its relations with China. However, Nepal continued to allow both India and Britain to recruit Gurkha soldiers for their armies.

53 China and Russia

The whole of northern Asia, from the Himalayas to the Arctic and from the Urals to the Pacific, was taken over by Russia and China in a series of conquests carried out from the 17th century to the 19th. The Chinese pushed west, the Russians east and south. Between them they subdued the Mongolians, the Tibetans, and all the region's Turkic-language peoples, ranging from the Azerbaijanis of the Caucasus to the Yakuts of eastern Siberia and including the Kazakhs, Turkmens, Uzbeks, Tartars, Tuvinians and Uighurs.

By the mid-19th century China's hold on Mongolia and on Chinese Turkestan (Xinjiang, or Sinkiang) was tenuous, and Tibet (52) was in practice independent. Meanwhile China had lost much territory to Russia. Russian colonists had been settled right across Siberia, to Yakutia and the Sea of Okhotsk, since the 17th century. In 1858 and 1860 the Russians annexed China's Pacific coast territory as far south as the border of Korea, near to which they built the port and naval base of Vladivostok – whose special value to them is that with icebreakers it can operate all year. The Russia–China frontier thus established in the Far East mainly followed the line of the upper Amur (Heilongjiang) river and its tributary the Ussuri.

In Central Asia, annexations between 1845 and 1895 advanced Russia's frontier from the Aral Sea to the present Soviet border. Part of the annexed area had once been within the Chinese empire, but at the time of the Russian conquest it was all held by independent Moslem states. China's weakness also enabled Russia to assert its influence in Xinjiang, Mongolia and north-east China (Manchuria). In 1898 Russia acquired a naval base in China, at Port Arthur (now part of the city of Lüda); Japan took over this base in 1905, Russia regained it in 1945, but in 1955 it was returned to China.

After Russia's 1917 revolutions the Turki peoples of Central Asia tried to regain their independence, but their revolts were suppressed. A million Kazakhs fled across the Chinese border to escape from Soviet rule, and millions of Russians were settled in Kazakhstan (where they now greatly outnumber the Kazakhs) and in the other nominally autonomous Central Asian republics of the USSR. In (Outer) Mongolia

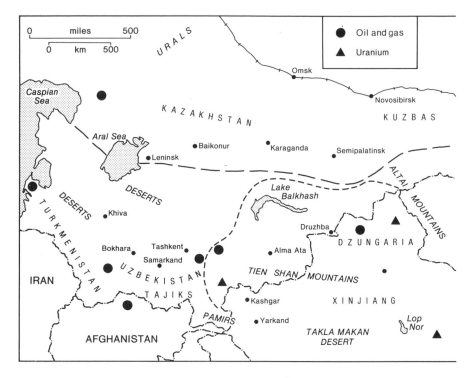

the Russians repelled China's attempts to regain control after 1917; Mongolia was declared independent in 1924, but Russia retained control and kept garrisons there. Tuvinia (Tannu-Tuva) was annexed by the USSR in 1944.

When Japan surrendered at the end of the 1939–45 war, Russia occupied north-east China (57), thus enabling the Chinese communists to make that region the main base from which they advanced to win the Chinese civil war in 1949. In the 1950s, although China and Russia were allies, their relations were not easy in the borderlands. Xinjiang ceased to be a Soviet sphere of influence. Millions of Chinese were settled in Xinjiang (hitherto peopled by Uighurs and Kazakhs) and in Inner Mongolia; in both regions the Chinese now outnumber the original inhabitants.

When open antagonism between Russia and China developed in the 1960s (7) the Chinese began to complain that parts of the frontier had been unjustly imposed by Russia. Tension rose on the border, and there were armed clashes, notably in 1969 near Druzhba in the west and at

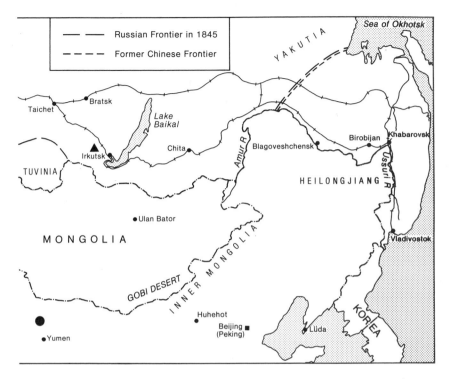

Russian Frontier in 1845

Former Chinese Frontier

Damansky (Chenpao) island in the Ussuri. The Russians, worried at the dangerous closeness to the border of the eastern part of their Trans-Siberian railway (built in 1891–1915, when a weak China posed no threat to it), began in the 1970s to build the 2000-mile Baikal–Amur railway farther to the north.

Both communist powers kept strong armed forces near the border. For both, Central Asia has provided sites for nuclear test explosions – China's near Lop Nor, Russia's at several places in Kazakhstan – and for missile test launchings. For both it is a source of uranium and oil. For Russia, the rapid population growth among the peoples of Central Asia is a cause of anxiety (*15*). But in 1979 the military value of its hold on this region was illustrated by its invasion of Afghanistan (*49*).

54 China and other neighbours

China, alone among nations, has more than 1000 million inhabitants; its armed forces are as big as Russia's, although less well equipped; it now has nuclear weapons and long-range missiles (*1, 4, 7, 10*). After a century of weakness which was exploited by Japan, Russia and several western states, China has again become the strongest power in the Far East. In 1949 the communists' victory in China's civil war made it an ally of Russia for a period during which it intervened in the Korean war (*58*) and supported the communist forces fighting in Indochina (*60*) and the less successful communist guerrillas in Malaya (*62*). Thailand and the Philippines were led to seek western support through SEATO, and other South-East Asian states became anxious about China's influence on the large Chinese minorities living within their borders (*59*).

Tensions in the region were somewhat reduced by China's break with the USSR and its rapprochement with the USA (*7, 53, 66*). China's new rulers seemed in no great hurry to make good their claims on Taiwan, Hongkong and Macao (*55, 56*). The only neighbour with which they came into large-scale violent conflict in the 1970s was communist-ruled Vietnam (*60, 61*).

Sea-zone claims (*6*) linked with hopes of oil in waters east and south of China seemed likely to foment new quarrels. Several groups of virtually uninhabited islands were involved: the Senkaku (Diaoyu) group, claimed by China, Taiwan and Japan; the Paracels (Xisha, or Hoang Sa), claimed by China and Vietnam (whose forces clashed there in 1982; in 1974 China had driven out a South Vietnam garrison); and the Spratlys (Nansha, or Truong Sa), claimed by China, Taiwan and Vietnam and in part by the Philippines – the last three states having all placed garrisons on islands in this scattered group.

On this map China's provinces and cities are given the spelling now officially approved in China. Some names (e.g. Yunnan, Shanghai) have not changed; for those that have, consult the index.

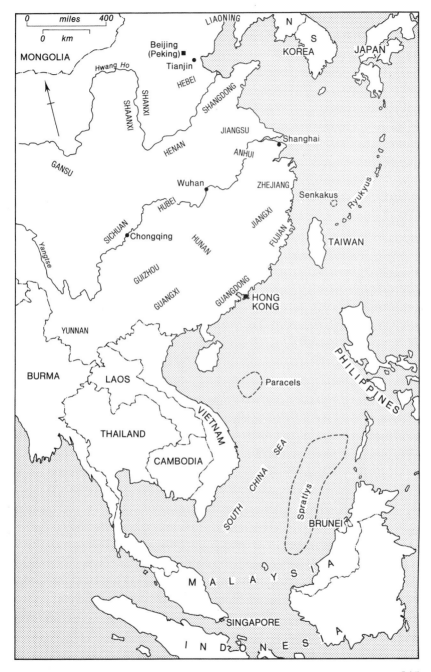

55 Taiwan

In 1949 China's defeated Nationalist (Kuomintang) government, headed by Chiang Kai-shek, took refuge in Taiwan (Formosa) after the communists' victory in the Chinese civil war. Taiwan, although ruled by Japan from 1895 to 1945, had for centuries been a Chinese province almost entirely populated by Chinese. In its present population of 18 million, less than a fifth are of recent mainland origin, but these mainlanders have remained dominant and the government has continued to insist that it is the rightful government of China. (It has been said that the only thing the two Chinas agree about is that there is only one China.) Until 1971 the government in Taipei held China's seat at the UN (8), but the 1970s saw the mainland government recognized by the great majority of other states, including the USA, so that Taiwan now has only informal relations with most countries. However, the American protection and support on which it has relied since 1949 has not been withdrawn, in spite of the mainland government's pressure on Washington, which has recently been concentrated on the question of continuing American supplies of arms to Taiwan.

In 1955 the Taiwan regime withdrew its forces from the Tachen islands, but it continued to maintain garrisons on Quemoy and Matsu (although the surrender of Quemoy in particular was repeatedly demanded, and it was heavily shelled from the mainland at times, notably in 1958). Taiwan has also retained control of the Pescadores (Penghu) and Pratas island (Tungsha), and it maintains a garrison on one of the islands in the Spratly group (54), where it has rejected claims made by the Philippines. It has – like mainland China and Japan – claimed the uninhabited Senkaku (Diaoyu) islands. Hopes of offshore oil are involved in this conflict of claims over small islands which are of no great importance in themselves.

The mainland Chinese rulers' attitude to Taiwan has always been that it must in due course be reunited with the rest of China; but they have seemed increasingly aware that simple integration could not appeal to its inhabitants – if only because they have achieved a higher standard of living than that of the mainland. Constitutional changes introduced in China in 1982 provided for 'special administrative regions'; this, it was

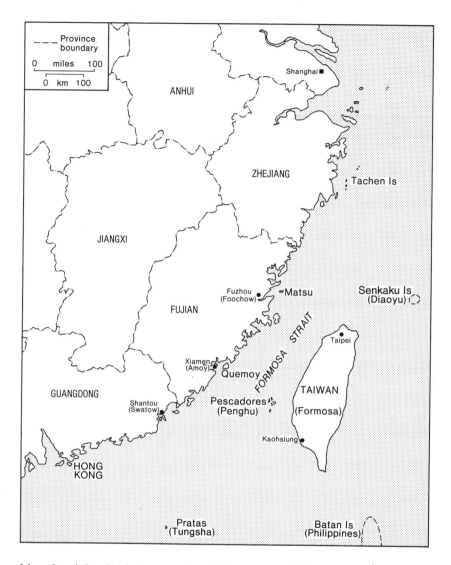

hinted, might allow the people of Taiwan – and Hongkong and Macao (56) – to retain some of their non-communist ways after being brought under the mainland regime's rule.

56 Hongkong

In the later part of the 19th century China's coast was speckled with small European-ruled enclaves – Russian, German, British, Portuguese and French. After 1955, when Russia relinquished its naval base at Port Arthur (Lüda – *53*), only Hongkong and Macao remained. Macao, where the Portuguese first settled in 1557, is no longer a major trading centre. During the 1960s effective control of it passed into Chinese hands, although it formally remained under Portuguese administration.

The island of Hongkong (on which the colony's capital, Victoria, stands) was ceded to Britain in 1842. The Kowloon area was similarly ceded in 1860, and in 1898 the New Territories were taken over from China on a lease running to 1997. Hongkong's population – which is 98% Chinese – has risen from $2\frac{1}{4}$ million in 1950 to about 5 million, largely because of huge influxes of refugees from the mainland since the communists' victory in the Chinese civil war (*55*). Some of Hongkong's entrepot trade was lost as a result of the upheavals in China, but it quickly became a new manufacturing centre.

Hongkong could not be successfully defended against any full-scale attack from the mainland, on which its crowded population depends for much of its normal food supplies and even of its water; and the island and Kowloon could not sustain a separate economy if the New Territories were transferred to Chinese control at the expiry of the lease. China's communist government has emphasized that it does not accept as valid any of the 'unequal treaties' under which Hongkong's territories were ceded or leased by previous Chinese governments, and that it intends eventually to take over the whole colony. However, Hongkong has been providing China with two-fifths of all its earnings of foreign exchange, and China has seemed more interested in profiting from Hongkong's economic activity than in destroying it. In 1979 China established 'special economic zones', adjacent to Hongkong and Macao, in which it encouraged foreign manufacturing and trading firms to start operating, taking advantage of low rents and wages and producing mainly for export. In 1982 constitutional changes were introduced in China which were apparently meant to signify that non-communist institutions might

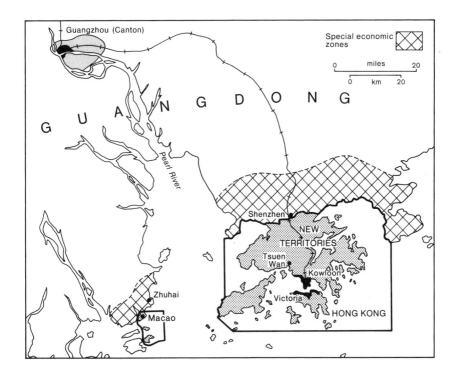

be preserved in Hongkong as well as in Taiwan (55). But doubts were voiced about Hongkong's ability to retain the confidence of investors as uncertainty about its future increased.

57 Japan's lost empire

Defeat in 1945 stripped Japan of an empire acquired in 50 years of conquest, which at its peak embraced most of the Far East. After several centuries of self-imposed isolation, Japan had embarked on a course of territorial expansion in 1895. By 1910 it had annexed Korea, taken Taiwan from China, and taken southern Sakhalin (Karafuto) from Russia. In 1919 it took over, under a League of Nations mandate, the Caroline, Mariana and Marshall islands, which had been a German colony. In 1931 it occupied Manchuria (the north-eastern region of China), where in 1932 it established a puppet state called Manchukuo. During the 1930s Japan conquered a large part of eastern China. In 1940 it occupied French Indochina (now Vietnam, Laos and Cambodia). In 1941 it occupied Thailand and, in a sweeping attack on all the American, British and Dutch territories in the Far East, Japanese forces were by mid-1942 in control of the Philippines, Guam and Wake Island; Hongkong, Malaya, Singapore, British Borneo and most of Burma; all of the Dutch East Indies (now Indonesia); much of New Guinea, most of the Solomons and all of the Gilbert islands; and, far to the north, the western Aleutians.

The earlier conquests were wiped out in 1945, as well as those of the 1941–45 Japanese war. China recovered Taiwan (*55*), and Russia recovered southern Sakhalin. Russia also seized the Kurile islands, and its troops occupied North Korea (*58*) and Manchuria until local communists had got a grip on those territories. American forces occupied South Korea (until 1949) and the Ryukyu and Bonin islands, as well as Japan itself, where Commonwealth troops joined them.

In the peace treaty concluded in 1951 with all the victorious allies of 1945 except Russia and China, Japan renounced its claims on Taiwan, Korea, Sakhalin and the Caroline, Mariana and Marshall islands. The allied occupation of Japan itself was ended; Japan made a mutual security treaty with the United States and gave it the right to keep forces in Japan for joint defence.

The Caroline, Mariana and Marshall islands became the American-administered Trust Territory of the Pacific Islands (often, for short, called Micronesia – *66*). In 1968 the Americans returned the Bonins and

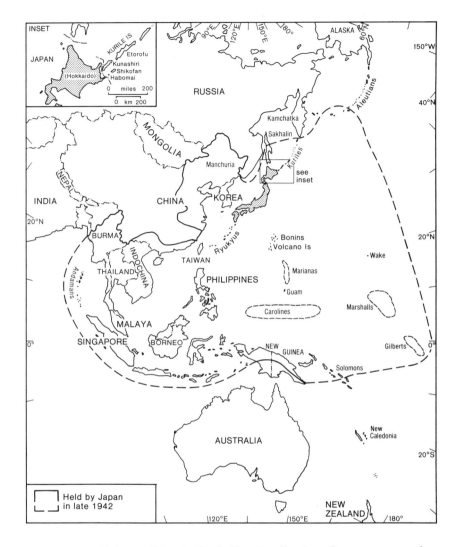

the adjacent Volcano Islands (including Iwojima) to Japanese control.
They similarly returned the northern Ryukyus in 1953 and the southern
Ryukyus (including Okinawa, where the USA retained rights to a base) in
1972.

Japan was at last able to sign a peace treaty with China in 1978. It had
signed no peace treaty with the USSR, partly because of a continuing
dispute over the Habomai, Shikotan, Kunashiri and Etorofu (Iturup)

islands, which lie near Hokkaido, the northernmost of Japan's main islands. Japan has long hoped to negotiate the return of these islands, which the Russians took over in 1945 along with the rest of the Kurile chain. A lesser dispute has arisen from the conflicting Japanese and Chinese claims to the Senkaku islands, near Taiwan (*54, 55*).

Japan's brief but spectacular phase of territorial conquests had been spurred on by the belief that a populous island nation, with few minerals and only limited farmland, must acquire overseas 'living space' and sources of raw materials. It was the oil, rubber, tin, iron ore and other minerals of South-East Asia that Japan's armed forces went south to seize in 1941–42. Yet it was only after 1945, when Japan was forced back to its pre-1895 territory, that it developed its economy so successfully that it became the world's third greatest power in economic terms (*2*). It has effectively curbed the growth of its population, and this has contributed to its high standard of living (*1*). It still depends heavily on oil imported mainly from the Middle East and on imports of minerals from many different regions (including Australia, Canada, India and South Africa). But its industrial strength and its importance as a market for countries that export raw materials have now gained it a position of great influence in the Far East and Pacific regions, and maintained it in that position far longer than its armies ever did.

58 Korea

Korea's history has largely been a story of competitive Chinese, Japanese and Russian efforts to dominate this relatively small nation almost surrounded by three bigger ones. For centuries China claimed Korea as a vassal state; but by the 1890s Japan and Russia were struggling to control it, and Japan, after defeating Russia in the 1904–5 war, took over Korea and held it until 1945 (*57*).

When Japan surrendered in 1945 American forces occupied southern Korea as well as Japan, and Russia (which had declared war on Japan a week before the surrender) occupied northern Korea as well as north-east China (Manchuria). It had been agreed that a united, free and democratic Korean state should be established, but in practice the Russians installed

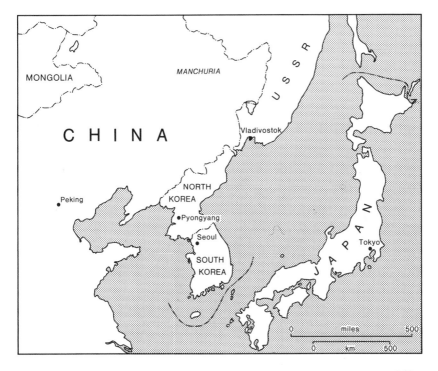

a communist regime in the north, suppressing all opposition; so elections were held in South Korea – which has more than two-thirds of the total population, now about 55 million – and a government was established in the national capital, Seoul. The American and Soviet forces withdrew, leaving the two states facing each other in hostility.

In June 1950 North Korea, which had been heavily armed by the Russians, invaded South Korea. Its forces broke through the much weaker South Korean ones and reached Seoul within 2 days. The United States at once sent troops to help resist the invasion, and the UN Security Council urged other nations to do the same. (No Soviet veto blocked this move – 8 – as Russia was then boycotting the council's meetings.) Altogether 16 nations sent men to fight in Korea under the UN flag. But at first only a few American and Commonwealth units could get there, and they and the South Koreans were forced back into the area around Pusan. There they held out until September, when fresh American forces landed at Inchon and cut the communist army's supply lines. The North Koreans were driven back across the 38th parallel, but they refused to make peace. The UN allies then advanced into the north, capturing Pyongyang.

When the UN forces approached the Chinese frontier, China sent into Korea a large army which drove south so far that Seoul once again fell into communist hands. By June 1951 the allies had fought their way back north of the 38th parallel again, China's army had suffered huge losses, and it agreed to negotiations; but these talks, held mainly at Panmunjom, dragged on until 1953, when an armistice was signed. (The main cause of delay was the communists' unsuccessful attempt to enforce the return of 50,000 prisoners of war who did not want to be sent back to China or North Korea.)

A peace conference in 1954 brought no agreement, and Korea remained divided along the 1953 armistice line. China's forces were withdrawn by 1958, and when China and Russia quarrelled in the 1960s (7, 53) North Korea, after at first tending to side with China, tried to become 'neutral' as between the two communist powers. It thus got some backing from each of them for its policy of maintaining pressure on South Korea (by sporadic raids as well as other tactics) and refusing to discuss reunification except on its own terms. This pressure from the north, and doubts about how long American protection against it would last, led South Korea, too, to maintain strong armed forces, which came to play a dominant role in its politics.

0   miles   100

0   km   100

USSR

Vladivostok

CHINA

Yalu R.

Chongjin

C

Antung

Sinuiju

Hungnam

Anju

PYONGYANG

Wonsan

Imjin R.

Kosong

E

Panmunjom   A

38° North

Inchon

SEOUL

D

B

Taegu

Kwangju

Pusan

Tsushima

Cheju (Quelpart)

JAPAN

A	Frontier 1945-50 (38th parallel)
B	Battlefront August 1950
C	Battlefront November 1950
D	Battlefront January 1951
E	Battlefront July 1951, Armistice line 1953, & present frontier

155

59 South-East Asia

Before the 1939–45 war, the only independent nation in South-East Asia was Thailand (called Siam until 1938, and again 1945–47). The rest of the region was under European or American rule: French in Indochina (Vietnam, Laos, Cambodia); Dutch in the East Indies (now Indonesia); British in Burma, Malaya and northern Borneo; American in the Philippines. Japan occupied Indochina in 1940 and overran the entire region in 1941–42 (*57*). In 1945 the Dutch were unable to regain full control of Indonesia, which later became an independent nation (*63*). The United States gave independence to the Philippines in 1946; Britain gave it to Burma in 1948 and to Malaya in 1957 (*62*). In Indochina the French faced a communist-led Vietnamese independence movement which, after the communists' victory in China's civil war, received strong support from China (*54, 60*).

By 1954 North Vietnam was being taken over by a communist regime, then backed by both China and Russia, which was also gaining footholds in Laos, Cambodia and South Vietnam. Communist guerrilla forces were active in Burma, Malaya and the Philippines, and all the South-East Asian countries were worried about the new strong China's influence on the large Chinese communities in the region. Thailand and the Philippines joined with Australia, Britain, France, New Zealand, Pakistan and the USA in signing the 1954 Manila treaty for South-East Asian defence, usually called SEATO. The SEATO allies agreed to act together against any attack in the region on one of them or on Cambodia, Laos or South Vietnam, although action on the territory of one of those three states would require its consent.

No joint defence action was taken under SEATO's formal authority, although American, Australian, New Zealand, Philippines and Thai forces went to fight in Vietnam in the 1960s (*60*). In the 1970s SEATO's activities were ended. Much had changed in the region since 1954. In Indochina military victory had gone to the communists; but Vietnam's communist rulers broke with China after 1975, siding with Russia against it. Meanwhile the South-East Asian states had formed a new grouping that was more truly regional than SEATO had been.

The Association of South-East Asian Nations (ASEAN) was formed

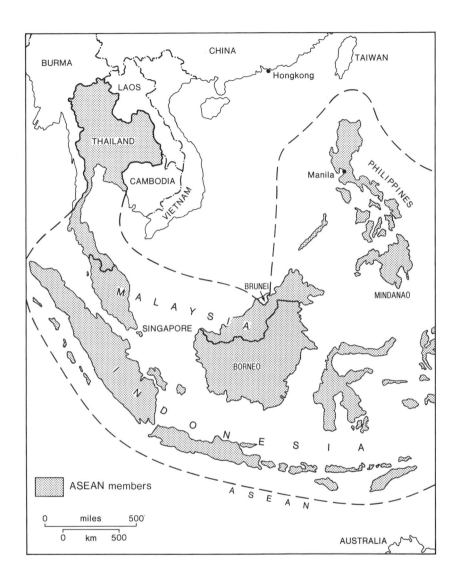

CHINA

BURMA

LAOS

Hongkong

TAIWAN

THAILAND

CAMBODIA

Manila

PHILIPPINES

VIETNAM

BRUNEI

MINDANAO

M A L A Y S I A

SINGAPORE

BORNEO

I N D O N E S I A

ASEAN members

A S E A N

0   miles   500

0   km   500

AUSTRALIA

in 1967 by Indonesia, Malaysia, Philippines, Singapore and Thailand. It was not designed as a military alliance, and while the Philippines and Thailand kept their defence links with the USA (66) the other ASEAN members preferred a 'non-aligned' course (7). But the five states developed a quite effective form of diplomatic co-operation, and in

157

1979–82 they worked together to prevent the Cambodian seat at the UN being taken over by the regime that Vietnam had installed in Cambodia (*61*).

A new problem for the region was created after 1975 by the flow of refugees from the three Indochina states, now all under communist rule. The largest number escaped into Thailand overland, but many (who became known as 'boat people') got out of Vietnam by sea in small craft. Those who survived these hazardous journeys found temporary asylum in the SEATO states, but these states demanded that the refugees should be resettled elsewhere. Western nations, notably the USA and France, took in many thousands, but over 40,000 'boat people' and 170,000 other refugees from Indochina were still in UN-aided camps in South-East Asia in 1982; 'boat people' were still fleeing from Vietnam at a rate of 100 a day; and the Cambodian refugees in Thailand did not seem likely to want to go back to Cambodia while it was occupied by a Vietnamese army which was contending with a guerrilla resistance.

The Philippines, Vietnam and China have been in dispute over some small islands in sea areas where hopes of offshore oil have revived old claims (*54*). In the southern Philippines, in Mindanao and the smaller islands south-west of it, the Moro (Moslem) rebellion that broke out in 1972 had not been completely extinguished in 1982. The country's Moslem minority (4% of a total population of 50 million) is concentrated in this region; its demands for more autonomy have found some support in Arab countries.

60 Indochina

Cambodia, Laos and Vietnam (Annam), three long-established kingdoms, all came under French rule between 1860 and 1900, forming French Indochina. During the 1940–45 Japanese occupation the communist-led Vietminh independence movement launched a guerrilla war in northern Vietnam (Tongking), and in 1945 it set up a government in Hanoi. From 1946 onwards there was fighting between the Vietminh and the French, while France began a transfer of power to non-communist governments in Cambodia and Laos as well as in Vietnam. In the early 1950s the Vietminh forces, which were now getting Chinese and Russian support, pressed their attacks in both Vietnam and Laos. In 1954, after they had trapped a French force at Dien Bien Phu, cease-fire agreements were signed. Vietnam was divided at the 17° North parallel; the French withdrew from North Vietnam, where the Vietminh again set up a government in Hanoi; in South Vietnam France completed the transfer of sovereignty to the government in Saigon. About 800,000 Vietnamese fled from north to south.

France also withdrew its forces from Cambodia and Laos, whose governments now had full sovereignty. In Laos the communists pulled back their forces into the north-eastern provinces; efforts were made to establish a 'neutral' coalition government with communist participation, but from 1959 onwards clashes multiplied and by 1961 the capital, Vientiane, was threatened by advancing communist troops. After a conference at Geneva, a new coalition was installed in 1962, but the confused struggles soon began again. Weak governments in Vientiane could not prevent North Vietnam using mountain tracks in eastern Laos to move arms and soldiers south and infiltrate them into South Vietnam from the west. Similar use was made of Cambodian territory.

By the early 1960s South Vietnam's government was losing control of many rural areas to guerrillas who were supplied, reinforced and directed from North Vietnam. The Americans, who since 1954 had given South Vietnam large-scale aid in the hope of checking the southward advance of communist power, became more directly involved in the struggle. In 1961, US 'combat advisers' were operating with South Vietnam units; by 1963 there were 16,000 US military personnel in Vietnam; in 1965 US aircraft began to bomb North Vietnam, and US ground forces arrived in the south; by 1968 there were 500,000 Americans there – and, alongside them and the South Vietnamese troops, there were contingents from Australia, New Zealand, the Philippines, South Korea and Thailand.

The Hanoi government's responses to offers of peace showed that it would accept nothing short of a communist take-over of South Vietnam; and this, in due course, it achieved. In 1969 the withdrawal of the American and allied forces began. In 1973 it was completed. A cease-fire was announced, but fighting soon became widespread again. During 1974 the North Vietnamese army fighting in the south became as large as South Vietnam's. By 1975 it was larger, and, advancing from the border areas which it had reached mainly through Laotian and Cambodian territory, it captured Saigon and the other southern cities. Vietnam was thus forcibly united under communist rule – which also meant rule by northerners. Saigon was renamed Ho Chi Minh City; southern communist leaders got no share of power; southern non-communists were hunted down, and a new refugee tide was set in motion (59).

After the fall of Saigon, Vientiane was quickly taken over by Laotian communists, supported and closely controlled by North Vietnamese ones. But in Cambodia the communist Khmers Rouges who captured Phnom Penh in 1975 were soon in dispute with Hanoi. They looked for help to China, which was becoming uneasy about having a heavily militarized and Soviet-backed Vietnam, with expansionist aims, as its neighbour. When Vietnam invaded Cambodia (61) at the end of 1978, China hit back by staging a limited invasion of Vietnam in February 1979; it captured several towns near the border, but withdrew its troops in March.

The occupation of Cambodia completed the conversion of Indochina into a Soviet sphere of influence. A special gain for Russia was that its fleet could now use bases at Camranh and Danang. This increased its naval capability in the Indian Ocean (41) as well as in the Far East.

C H I N A

Caobang •

• Laocai

Red River

Langson •

• Dien Bien Phu

HANOI

Mekong

• Luang Prabang

Gulf of Tongking

River

Hainan
(China)

V I E T N A M

• Vientiane

• Udon Thani

17° North

L A O S

Savannakhet •

Hué •

• Danang

T H A I L A N D

Ubon •

Mekong R.

• Kontum

■ BANGKOK

C A M B O D I A

Battambang •

Tonle Sap
Lake

Camranh

Dalat •

PHNOM PENH

• Kompong
Som

SAIGON
■ (Ho Chi Minh City)

Mekong Delta

0   miles   150

0   km   150

161

61 Cambodia

Cambodia (Kampuchea) is the remnant of the old Khmer kingdom which once included southern Vietnam and part of Siam (Thailand). After losing the Mekong delta to the Vietnamese, Cambodia was dominated alternately by Vietnam and Siam until it became a French protectorate in 1863. Unlike Laos, it has no mountain frontier separating it from Vietnam, and there is a tradition of antagonism between these neighbours. In the 1960s the Cambodians tried to keep clear of the conflicts in Vietnam and Laos, and they turned a blind eye to North Vietnam's use of Cambodian border regions as transit routes and bases for its forces attacking South Vietnam (60); but in 1970 Cambodia itself became a battlefield, with American and South Vietnam forces supporting those of the government in Phnom Penh against the North Vietnamese and the Cambodian communist guerrillas ('Khmers Rouges'). As in South Vietnam, the communist forces got the upper hand when American support for the government was withdrawn, and in 1975 they captured Phnom Penh two weeks before the fall of Saigon.

Cambodia's new communist rulers quickly became notorious for their ineptness and cruelty. They cleared Phnom Penh and other cities of their inhabitants, asserting that the whole population must work in the fields; in practice, the result was mass starvation and a surge of refugees across the border into Thailand. Meanwhile the old enmity between the Indochinese states was revived and embittered by the fact that the Khmers Rouges refussto follow Vietnam in toeing the Soviet line; they looked instead to China. Clashes on the border became serious in 1977 and multiplied during 1978. Vietnam launched a full-scale invasion of Cambodia in December 1978. In January 1979 its forces captured Phnom Penh and installed there a government which was entirely dependent on Vietnam. (China retaliated by mounting an invasion of Vietnam – 60). In spite of the appalling experience of rule by the Khmers Rouges, the Cambodians did not welcome the Vietnamese invaders as liberators, and Vietnam had to deploy a large army of occupation to hold the country down and protect the new government in Phnom Penh.

Vietnam's conquest of Cambodia was condemned by most third-world states as well as by western ones. It caused alarm throughout South-East

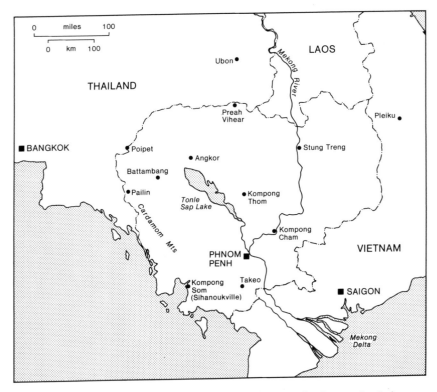

Asia, particularly in Thailand (from which US forces had been withdrawn in 1976). More Cambodian refugees poured into Thailand; there were about 300,000 there in 1982, mostly in camps near the border. Much of the 150,000-strong Vietnamese army of occupation was sent to areas near the Thai border, where both the Khmers Rouges and new non-communist guerrilla forces were active. In 1980–82 the Vietnamese troops repeatedly crossed the Thai border during their campaigns against the guerrillas; most of these frontier violations occurred east and north of Battambang. In 1982 the Cambodian resistance movements announced their formation of a coalition government. Although it did not control much territory inside Cambodia, it got a good deal of international backing, notably from the ASEAN states (59).

62 Malaysia and Singapore

Malaysia, with its federal capital at Kuala Lumpur, comprises the sultanates of mainland Malaya (with Penang island), and the Borneo states of Sabah (formerly British North Borneo) and Sarawak. Five-sixths of the 14 million inhabitants live in West Malaysia (the mainland). The majority are Malays (who are mostly Moslems), but about 33% are Chinese and 9% Indians.

Malaya (the mainland) became an independent federation in 1957, after a long period of British rule interrupted by the Japanese occupation in 1942–45. The guerrilla and terrorist campaign that communist Chinese in Malaya had launched in 1948 was not completely defeated until 1960, but democratic elections were held regularly from 1955 onward, producing federal governments based on an alliance between Malay, Chinese and Indian parties.

Singapore, an island of only 225 square miles, developed during 140 years of British rule into a major port and industrial centre, with a British naval base until 1971. It now has $2\frac{1}{2}$ million inhabitants, three-quarters of them Chinese. In 1963, together with Sabah and Sarawak, it joined Malaya in the enlarged federation, which was named Malaysia. But the mainland Malays were never really happy about taking this large Chinese element into the federation. In 1965 Singapore was obliged to withdraw, and it became a separate independent republic.

The sultanate of Brunei in north Borneo chose not to join Malaysia in 1963, and remained under British protection. (Later, it was agreed that it would become fully independent in 1983.) Brunei, with a population of only 220,000, was formerly distinguished by its possession of a rich oilfield, but more recently offshore discoveries made Malaysia also an oil exporter.

Indonesia angrily opposed the inclusion of Sabah and Sarawak in Malaysia in 1963, even after UN investigations had confirmed that the inhabitants of those former British territories wanted to join the federation; for the next 2 years Indonesia carried on a campaign of 'confrontation', including border raids (*63*). In 1968–69 the Philippines briefly revived an ancient claim to Sabah. Malaysia was more seriously

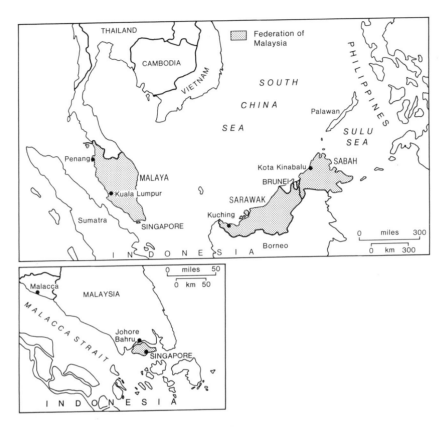

troubled in 1969 by race riots, in which its Chinese inhabitants were attacked by Malays who were both influenced by Islamic fundamentalism (*28*) and resentful of the relative prosperity of some of the Chinese.

63 Indonesia and New Guinea

In 1945 Holland was unable to restore its authority over the Dutch East Indies, which Japan had seized in 1942. An independent republic, initially controlling only some parts of Java and Sumatra, was proclaimed. Its leaders negotiated with the Dutch, but in 1947 fighting became widespread. The United Nations obtained a cease-fire, sent military observers to ensure compliance, and provided a 'good offices' committee which helped to get an agreed transfer of sovereignty in 1949. The new independent Indonesia included all the former Dutch East Indies except West Irian (the western half of New Guinea), which remained under Dutch rule.

Indonesia's demands for the handing over of West Irian mounted; in 1962 its forces began to attack the territory, and the Dutch agreed to transfer it. A temporary UN administration, backed by a small UN force,

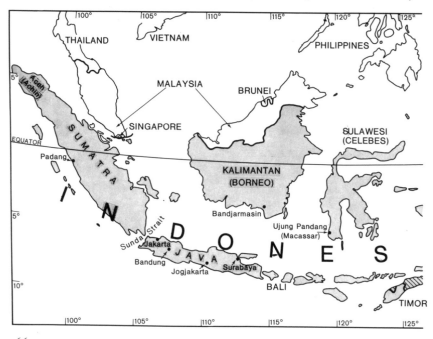

eased the transition by taking charge of West Irian for a few months, and Indonesian rule there began in 1963. It had been agreed that the territory's 800,000 inhabitants should be asked by 1969 whether they wanted Indonesian rule. When 1969 came there were risings, and many people fled into eastern New Guinea; but Indonesia produced a rather dubious show of support by groups supposedly representative of the people of the territory (now called Irian Jaya).

Of Indonesia's 150 million inhabitants, some 90 million are crowded into Java. Relations between the various islands have at times been strained. One local problem, in this mainly Moslem country, has been that of Ambon (Amboina) and the neighbouring South Moluccan islands, one of the earliest areas of European colonization; thousands of Christian Ambonese went to Holland after 1949, and some groups continued to demand separate independence for the South Moluccas. A more widespread problem is that of the three million Chinese who have often been made scapegoats at times of trouble.

Between 1963 and 1965 Indonesia tried to prevent the formerly British parts of Borneo from joining the new Malaysian federation (62). Its 'confrontation' tactics included guerrilla attacks across the border, and

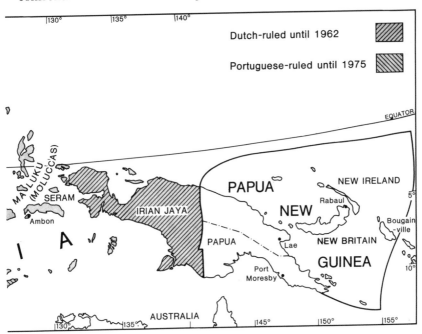

even some on mainland Malaya; these attacks were repelled with the help of British forces.

In 1975 Indonesia seized East Timor, the only territory in the East Indies that Portugal had retained after it lost control of the region to the Dutch more than 300 years ago. As soon as the end of Portuguese rule seemed imminent, fighting had started in East Timor between pro-Indonesian groups and those who wanted independence. Indonesia's forces suppressed the independence movement (Fretilin) with a brutality that alienated more of the Timorese and caused further resistance. It was feared that the conflict, and the consequent famine and disease, might have cost as many as 100,000 lives by 1982 – in a territory whose total population had been less than 700,000.

Papua New Guinea (the eastern half of New Guinea, with the adjacent islands) became independent in 1975. Previously its southern part (the Territory of Papua) was an Australian dependency, and the north – with the islands, including Bougainville in the northern Solomons – was an Australian-administered UN trust territory (it had been held by Germany from 1884 to 1914, and occupied by Japan in 1942–44). In 1975 there were separatist agitations in Bougainville – whose copper mines provide large revenues – and in some other areas, but they abated when decentralizing measures were introduced. A different problem for Papua New Guinea arose from border-crossings by Indonesian forces in pursuit of guerrillas who were still resisting Indonesian rule in western New Guinea. Whatever feelings of sympathy the people of 'PNG' might have for their western neighbours (and, sometimes, kinsfolk), the new state's small armed forces could not possibly control its long land frontier. On the other hand, in 1980 a small contingent of soldiers from PNG was able to give decisive help to the government of newly independent Vanuatu by ending the secessionist rebellion on Espiritu Santo island. This action and others have brought out the fact that Papua New Guinea, although overshadowed by its big neighbour Indonesia to the west, now looms quite large itself in relation to the smaller Pacific islands to its east (65).

64 Australia and New Zealand

These two nations, separated by 1000 miles of the Tasman Sea, are isolated but also shielded by wide oceans on three sides. Mainly peopled from Britain, they at first relied on British naval protection; and in 1914 and again in 1939 they rallied to Britain's side in war, sending troops to fight in Europe and the Middle East. But in 1942 they themselves faced a threat from the north: Japan's forces, advancing by way of the south-east Asian archipelagos, were stopped only when they had seized most of New Guinea and reached the Solomons. Australia and New Zealand made a defence treaty with the USA (ANZUS) in 1951, joined in signing the SEATO treaty in 1954, and sent forces to Korea and Malaya in the 1950s and to Vietnam in the 1960s (*58–62, 66*). For defence, they now look ultimately to the American alliance, much as they once looked to Britain. They have also sought to cultivate connections with south Asian countries (and with the small Pacific island states) and to take a more active part in the whole region's affairs than they did in the days when their links with Britain still dominated their outlook.

Today, most of the 15 million Australians are townspeople; nine million of them live in the five biggest cities, which are all on the coast of this huge country; much of the interior is desert or very arid land. An economy which had been mainly pastoral has been rapidly transformed, particularly by discoveries of great mineral wealth (*5*). Enough coal, oil,

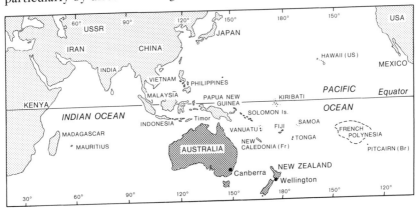

gas and uranium has been found to make Australia an important exporter of fuels. The map indicates the main sources of certain minerals; others, not marked, include copper, gold, tin and tungsten. Much of the mining output is exported, Japan being a major customer, but what is retained and processed in Australia has served to build up steel, chemical and other industries. Farming, however, still provides a large share of exports, especially wheat, wool, meat and sugar.

New Zealand has not enjoyed such a mining bonanza. Its wool, meat and butter still make up three-fifths of its exports. It has found coal, gas and a certain amount of oil, and has been able to exploit important hydro-electric and geothermal energy resources. Its industries are mostly on a small scale, but two-thirds of its 3.2 million inhabitants now live in the main urban areas. It had to struggle to diversify its overseas trade when Britain, which was taking more than half of its exports as recently as the 1960s, joined the EEC (*19*), whose protectionist farm policies had the effect of halving New Zealand's sales of butter to Britain. Australia, Japan, the USA and Britain became of roughly equal importance as markets for New Zealand, taking between them about half of all its exports.

The 1965 New Zealand–Australia Free Trade Agreement (NAFTA) was aimed at encouraging the growth of trade across the Tasman Sea, mainly by reducing certain tariffs. In 1982 the two countries completed long negotiations for a more far-reaching CER (closer economic relations) agreement, under which nearly all tariffs and import restrictions on trade between them were to be removed by stages.

In Australia only 1% of the population is of Aboriginal or part-Aboriginal descent; but about 9% of New Zealanders are of at least half Maori (Polynesian) origin, and there has also been some recent immigration of other Polynesian islanders, especially from the Cook Islands and Niue, former dependencies now self-governing but still in association with New Zealand, and Western Samoa, a former trust territory now fully independent (*65*).

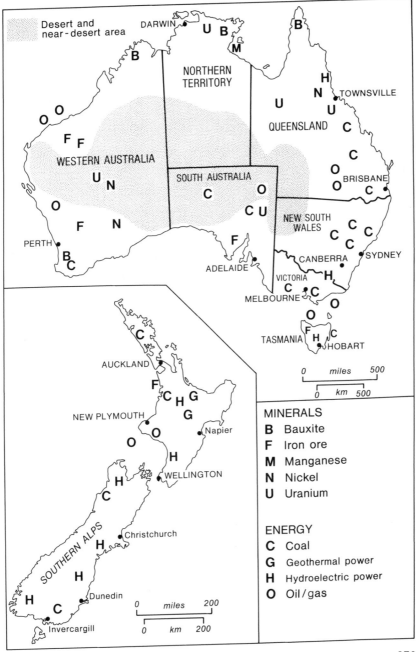

Desert and near-desert area

DARWIN

U B
M

NORTHERN TERRITORY

B

QUEENSLAND

TOWNSVILLE

H
N
U

C

C

O O BRISBANE
C

O O

F F

WESTERN AUSTRALIA

U N

SOUTH AUSTRALIA

C

O
C U

NEW SOUTH WALES

C C
C C

SYDNEY

O

F N

PERTH

B
C

F

ADELAIDE

CANBERRA

VICTORIA
C C
MELBOURNE

H

O

O

TASMANIA

F H C
HOBART

0 miles 500

0 km 500

AUCKLAND

C

F
C H G
G

NEW PLYMOUTH

O O

Napier

H

WELLINGTON

C
H

SOUTHERN ALPS

Christchurch

H

H

H C

Dunedin

Invercargill

0 miles 200

0 km 200

MINERALS

B Bauxite
F Iron ore
M Manganese
N Nickel
U Uranium

ENERGY

C Coal
G Geothermal power
H Hydroelectric power
O Oil/gas

65 South Pacific

By 1982 tiny Pitcairn was the only British dependency in the region. Between 1970 and 1980, Fiji, Kiribati, the Solomon Islands, Tonga and Tuvalu had become independent (9). Kiribati and Tuvalu were formerly the Gilbert and Ellice Islands; Banaba, or Ocean Island, was included in Kiribati after negotiations with the 2000 Banabans, who had sought separate independence. (They were then living on a Fijian island while their own island's phosphates were excavated.)

French Polynesia, New Caledonia, and Wallis and Futuna were still French overseas territories in 1982, but Melanesian pressure for independence had mounted in New Caledonia (a major source of nickel – 5), which has a large European minority. In 1980 the British–French condominium of the New Hebrides became independent as Vanuatu, with an elected government headed by English-speaking Melanesians, in

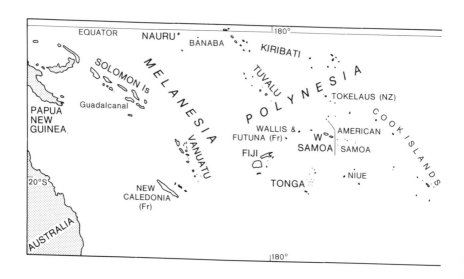

spite of an attempt at secession by French-speakers on Espiritu Santo island. Vanuatu called in troops from Papua New Guinea to help suppress this revolt (*63*). Nauru and Western Samoa, formerly administered respectively by Australia and New Zealand, are now independent (*8, 9*). The Cook Islands and Niue are self-governing in association with New Zealand; the Tokelaus are an NZ territory.

The South Pacific pattern is one of small populations on small islands scattered across vast areas of sea. (The biggest concentration of people is in Fiji – about 650,000, half of them descended from immigrants who came from India in the period 1880–1920.) But even small islands can now claim large sea areas (*6*) and make foreigners pay for the right to fish in them; this may strengthen some of the region's weakest economies.

The island governments and those of Australia and New Zealand meet regularly in the South Pacific Forum. Its members have signed a trade agreement (Sparteca) which gives many island exports favoured access to the Australian and NZ markets. Forum members have urged France to respond to New Caledonian and Polynesian demands for early independence and to stop staging nuclear tests at Mururoa (*10*).

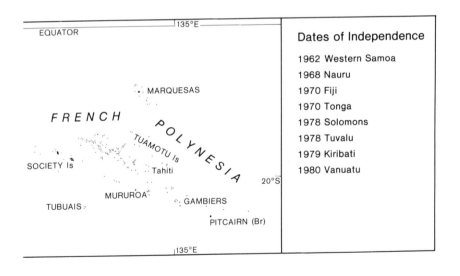

EQUATOR — 135°E

MARQUESAS

FRENCH

TUAMOTU Is

POLYNESIA

SOCIETY Is

Tahiti

20°S

MURUROA

GAMBIERS

TUBUAIS

PITCAIRN (Br)

135°E

Dates of Independence

1962 Western Samoa
1968 Nauru
1970 Fiji
1970 Tonga
1978 Solomons
1978 Tuvalu
1979 Kiribati
1980 Vanuatu

66 America and the Pacific

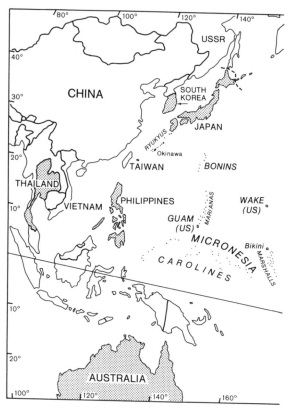

In the 19th century the Americans reached out into and across the Pacific. They bought Alaska, including the Aleutian islands, from Russia in 1867; they took the Philippines and Guam from Spain (1898), and annexed Midway (1867), Hawaii (1898), Wake Island (1898), and eastern Samoa (1899; they had obtained the Pago Pago naval base there in 1878). Between 1904 and 1914 they built the Panama Canal (6, 70), which gave merchant ships and warships a shorter route between Atlantic and Pacific than the one round Cape Horn (72). In Japan, whose rulers had long discouraged foreign contacts, the Americans' opening up of the country to trade (1854) had fateful consequences; later, the USA tried to protect China against European and Japanese encroachments (54); later still, it became more and more worried about Japan's ambitions – which eventually led to the 1941 Japanese attack on the Philippines and on the US naval base at Pearl Harbor, on Oahu island in the Hawaiian group. As

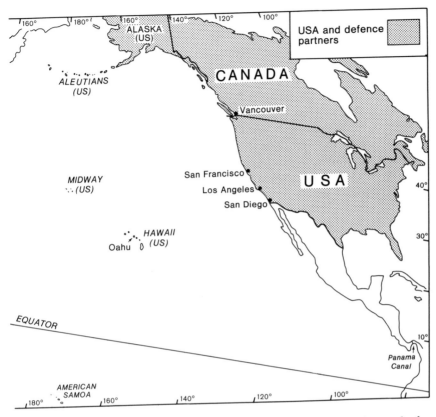

well as the Philippines, Japan also seized Guam, Wake and the westernmost Aleutians (*57*).

After the Americans had fought their way back across the Pacific and Japan had surrendered in 1945, they became heavily committed to protecting countries and areas along the ocean's western shores. The invasion of South Korea in 1950 and the successes of the communist forces in Indochina during the 1950s aroused widespread fears about the new power of a communist-ruled China which then had strong Soviet backing (*54, 58–60*). The United States undertook to protect Taiwan against attack from the Chinese mainland (*55*) and South Korea against any renewed attack from the north; and it was drawn deeper and deeper into the conflict in Vietnam (*60*).

In 1951 it joined Australia and New Zealand in the Pacific Security Treaty (often called the ANZUS treaty – *64*), and signed a security treaty with Japan, which agreed to allow American forces to be stationed in Japan to help defend it. In 1954 the three ANZUS allies, with Britain, France, Pakistan, the Philippines and Thailand, signed the SEATO treaty for collective defence in South-East Asia (59); during the 1970s SEATO ended its activity and the US bases in Thailand were closed, but the Philippines and Thailand still have defence arrangements with the USA (and Pakistan turned to it for military aid after Russia's 1979 occupation of Afghanistan – 49). The whole situation in the Pacific region was affected during the 1960s and 1970s by the rift between China and Russia; the American rapprochement with China; the communists' military victories in Indochina; and the bitter feelings which the war in Vietnam aroused among Americans, moving them to withdraw from that struggle and recoil from the idea of involvement in any other conflict of a similar kind (53, 55, 60). However, in 1982 the USA was still extensively committed to the defence of states on the western side of the Pacific, and these commitments still seemed essential for the stability of the region.

The United States gave independence to the Philippines in 1946. Between 1953 and 1972 it returned the Ryukyu, Bonin and Volcano islands, which it had occupied in 1945, to Japanese control (57). In 1959 Alaska and Hawaii, previously dependent territories, became the 49th and 50th of the United States. Guam and American Samoa are US territories, as are Midway, Wake and several other small Pacific islands which have no permanent populations.

The Carolines, Marianas (excluding Guam) and Marshalls, which Japan had held under a League of Nations mandate (before 1914, they were German colonies), became, in 1947, the American-administered Trust Territory of the Pacific Islands – often called Micronesia. Unlike other UN trust territories (8), this one was given 'strategic' status; Bikini and Eniwetok, both in the Marshalls, were used for American nuclear tests in the 1950s, and more recently missile test firings from California have been directed at the waters near Kwajalein in the Marshalls. Micronesia's 150,000 people live on hundreds of small islands scattered over 3 million square miles of sea. In 1978 the Northern Marianas became a commonwealth associated with the USA in a relationship similar to that of Puerto Rico (70); in 1980 an agreement was concluded for the granting of autonomy to the Marshalls, and similar arrangements were proposed for the Palau (Belau) islands and the remaining parts of Micronesia, with the aim of terminating the trusteeship within a few years.

67 United States of America

The American frontiers with Canada and Mexico had taken their present form by 1853. From 1912, when Arizona attained statehood, there were 48 states; in 1959 Alaska and Hawaii (66), formerly US territories, became the 49th and 50th states. Within these borders the American population has both grown and moved in impressive numbers.

Since 1930, when it was 123 million, it has almost doubled and is now over 230 million. About 13 million immigrants have been admitted since 1930; immigration is running at about 500,000 a year (precise figures are hard to establish because of large-scale illegal entry, particularly from Mexico). Although the United States was mainly peopled from Europe, and its immigration quotas were long designed to preserve the population mix, the proportion of immigrants coming from other parts of the world has sharply increased.

The total population now includes about 15 million people of Hispanic American origin (largely from Mexico and Puerto Rico – 70); about 800,000 American Indians; and about 27 million 'blacks', partly or wholly of African origin. The south-eastern states (the 'Old South') contained 85% of the blacks in 1920, and 60% of them as recently as 1960; but less than half of them live there now. There has been a massive black migration to the big cities of the north and the far west; in the late 1960s many of those cities were afflicted with race riots, against a background of unrest that also reflected the tensions caused by American involvement in the Vietnam war (60). Blacks now make up a third or more of the population of such cities as Chicago, Cleveland and Detroit.

However, there has been an even larger movement of people in the opposite direction – away from the north-east and north-central ('Midwest') regions. Those regions had long contained more than half of the total population (they still contain most of the big cities). In 1970 they still had 8 million more inhabitants than the south and west; now the balance has tipped the other way. New York, the most populous state until the 1960s, has been overtaken by California (24 million). The 'centre of gravity' of population has, for the first time, moved to the western side of the Mississippi. There are political implications: the south and west now elect more than half of the House of Representatives.

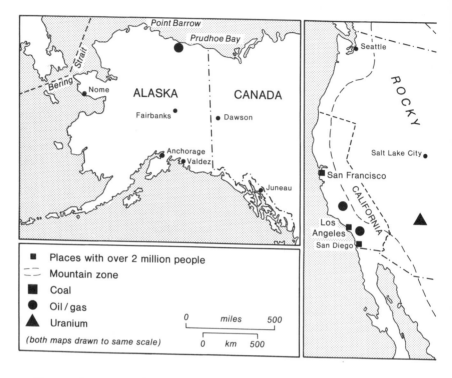

Economic power, too, has shifted away from the northern regions, where it formerly rested on their resources of coal, iron ore, and (in earlier days) oil. The coalfields are still important; steel plants near the Great Lakes can now use iron ore shipped from eastern Canada and farther afield, thanks to the St Lawrence Seaway, opened in 1959 (*68*); but the industrializing of the south and west has been speeded up by the exploiting of hydroelectric power, oil and natural gas.

Alaskan oil, piped from the North Slope to Valdez and thence moved in tankers, now provides a fifth of American oil supplies. Oil and gas from western Canada come south by pipeline, and there are plans for longer pipelines to bring gas from Alaska and the Canadian Arctic. These developments have helped to reduce American dependence on oil from the Middle East and other regions of potential instability; but the United States, despite its own huge production, is still a major oil importer. During the 1970s its use of nuclear energy was still growing, but by the early 1980s this growth had been sharply checked – partly by anxiety about the safety of nuclear power plants, which was particularly aroused

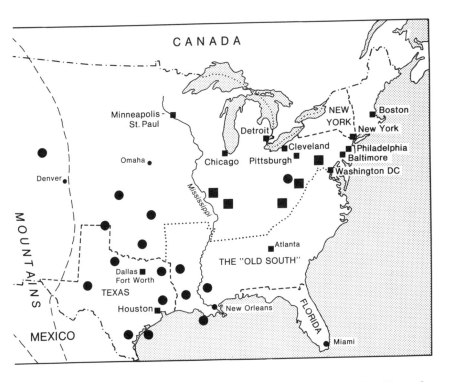

by the 1979 accident at the Three Mile Island reactor near Harrisburg in Pennsylvania, 100 miles west of Philadelphia (*3*, *4*).

Since the 1920s and 1930s, when 'isolationism' was strong enough to keep the United States out of the League of Nations, its international position has been transformed. For more than 30 years it has kept forces in Germany, Japan and elsewhere and has seen countries in Europe and on the western side of the Pacific look to it for support – without always agreeing with its policies (*7*, *10*, *20*, *59*, *66*). It has also come to play a major part in the affairs of the Middle East (*42–47*) and has had to give increasing attention to the Central American and Caribbean regions, where its influence is no longer unchallenged (*70*).

68 Canada

In 1982 Canada at last completed its constitution (which dated from 1867) by adopting a formula for amending it. Until then, because the federal government and the ten provincial ones could not agree on an amending formula, each change had to be approved by Britain – although Canada had long been a fully independent nation in other respects. The controversy that preceded the 1982 reform was a new chapter in the long story of disputes about Canada's national unity.

That unity has always been a defiance of both geography and history. Nearly all the 24 million Canadians live in a 3000-mile-long strip of territory bordering the United States; but, despite strong American economic and cultural influences, they have insisted on maintaining their separate identity. Yet Canada itself is bicultural. It originated from British and French colonies, and its official languages are English and French. Today about 30% of the population speaks French. Only 45% of Canadians are of British or Irish origin, but immigrants of other origins have mostly chosen to learn English.

Quebec is the only province where French Canadians form a majority; they make up four-fifths of its population of $6\frac{1}{2}$ million. In New Brunswick they are about two-fifths; elsewhere they make up only a tenth or less of the populations of Ontario ($8\frac{3}{4}$ million), the four western provinces ($6\frac{1}{2}$ million), and the Atlantic ones ($2\frac{1}{4}$ million for the four, including New Brunswick). Some French Canadians have sought to defend French language rights throughout the country in order to preserve a united and bicultural Canada. Others think this a lost cause, and argue that French culture must be defended in its one stronghold, Quebec – if necessary, by separating it from the rest of Canada.

In the late 1960s and early 1970s Quebec separatism was encouraged by gestures from France – which strained relations between the governments in Paris and Ottawa. The 1976 provincial election in Quebec brought a separatist-minded party to power there. It met a setback in 1980 when only half of the province's French-speakers backed its 'sovereignty-association' ideas in a referendum, but this did not dispose of the issue, and feeling became heated again in Quebec when the 1982 constitutional reform left the province without the power to veto future changes in the federal constitution.

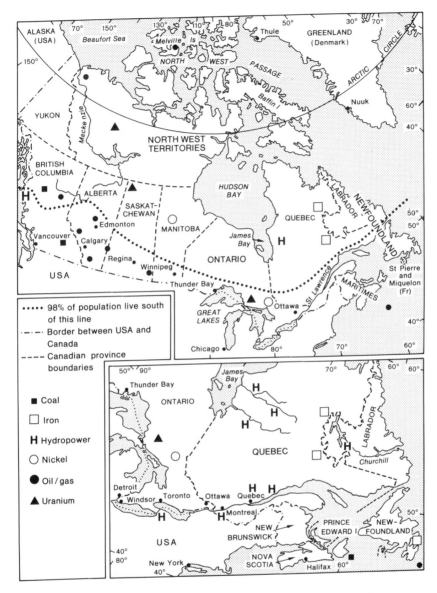

Meanwhile, the federal government's moves in the 1960s and 1970s to avert a secession by restoring the status of the French language and taking more account of Quebec's complaints had caused friction between Ottawa and the western provinces, which had their own complaints about

181

the predominance of 'the east' – meaning Ontario as well as Quebec. There were even some separatist rumblings in the west, whose oil and other mineral resources had brought rapid economic development (with oil and gas from Alberta, potash from Saskatchewan and nickel from Manitoba flowing to the United States, and coal from British Columbia to Japan).

The recent weakness of the oil market and the international recession (3) have led to a slowing down of projects in several regions of Canada, including: extraction of oil from the Athabaska tar sands in northern Alberta; the building of pipelines to bring gas south from Alaska and the neighbouring Canadian regions; the use of the North West Passage by icebreaking tankers bringing out Arctic oil and liquefied gas; and the exploitation of newly found oil and gas fields off the shores of Newfoundland and Nova Scotia. These energy resources, however, are potentially very large. Quebec, lacking oil or gas, has harnessed the rivers flowing into James Bay for a huge hydroelectric scheme which provides surplus power for export to the USA as well as to Ontario.

Newfoundland joined the Canadian federation as recently as 1949. Close to its coast lie the small islands of St Pierre and Miquelon, which form a French overseas *département* with a population of only 6000. There are rich fisheries in these waters, and Canada and France have for some years been in dispute about fishing rights. Canadian–US disputes over similar issues arose in the 1970s when both countries claimed 200-mile-wide sea zones off their coasts (6).

69 Latin America

Brazil represents what was once Portugal's empire in the Americas. The 18 Hispanic republics – including two in the Caribbean (Cuba and the Dominican Republic) – represent Spain's former empire there. Haiti was once a French possession. These 20 Latin republics, together with the United States, were members of the Pan-American Union, which was succeeded in 1948 by the Organization of American States (OAS). Since the 1960s, the OAS has suspended Cuba (70) from membership and has been joined by nine ex-British Caribbean states and by Surinam. The 1947 Rio Treaty (formally, Inter-American Treaty of Reciprocal Assistance) was ratified by the 20 Latin states, the US and Trinidad; it provided for joint action if any member was attacked. Argentina invoked the Rio Treaty during the 1982 Falklands conflict (73). It got little response; but American opposition to Argentina's invasion of the islands increased the feeling in Latin America that the OAS was excessively US-dominated.

Moves for economic integration in the region have had only partial success. In 1960 the Latin American Free Trade Association (LAFTA) was founded by Mexico and the ten Latin states of South America. It made little progress towards creating a common market, and in 1980 the same 11 states agreed to relaunch the effort, replacing LAFTA with the new Latin American Integration Association (LAIA). Five Central American states – Costa Rica, Guatemala, Honduras, Nicaragua, El Salvador – which had formed a political grouping, OCAS, in 1951, tried to create a common market in the 1960s but this effort, too, petered out. In 1969 the Andean Pact was signed by Bolivia, Chile, Colombia, Ecuador and Peru (joined in 1973 by Venezuela). This group adopted rules about foreign investment, and encouraged specialization in production, but it was weakened by Chile's withdrawal in 1974. In the Caribbean, the ex-British states launched a free trade association in the 1960s and in 1973 expanded it into the Caribbean Community (Caricom), with diplomatic and political functions as well as economic ones. By 1982 Caricom had 13 member states and showed many signs of vitality, although Grenada (71) was posing problems for a group whose members were mostly upholding democratic freedoms.

183

One of the obstacles to regional unity is the persistence of old territorial disputes. OAS mediation has averted or moderated several conflicts of this kind, and there has been no recent war comparable to the long one that Bolivia and Paraguay fought in 1932–35 (the 'Chaco war', so named from the disputed territory; Paraguay got most of it, but at a fearful cost in lives and money). But Argentina and Chile have an old quarrel over the Beagle Channel islands (72, 73); Colombia has one with Nicaragua, and one with Venezuela, which in turn has claims on Guyana (70, 71).

In 1942, after a short war, Ecuador had to cede territory to Peru; in 1961 it declared that it would no longer respect the 1942 treaty; in 1981, after a series of incidents, there was a 5-day conflict followed by an uneasy cease-fire. Originally, Ecuador's complaint was that it had been denied access to the Amazon river's upper reaches; the reviving of the dispute was linked with both countries' searches for oil.

Bolivia has hoped to regain an outlet to the sea ever since Chile defeated Bolivia and Peru in the 'War of the Pacific' (1879–83) and took from them the mineral-rich coastal area running south from Arica. In 1975 Chile offered to cede to Bolivia a narrow 'corridor' running to the sea just north of Arica; but Peru objected that Chile was bound by treaty not to give away this territory without Peru's consent; and Bolivia was hesitant about accepting Chile's terms, which included a demand for an area in the south-west corner of Bolivia. The 1975 deal lapsed, and Bolivia broke off diplomatic relations with Chile; they had not been resumed in 1982.

The 1967 Treaty of Tlatelolco (named from a mountain near Mexico City) was designed to make Latin America a zone free of nuclear weapons. But it was still not in full force, 15 years later, in regard to Argentina, Brazil, Chile or Cuba.

USA

MEXICO

Bermuda (Br)

GUATEMALA
EL SALVADOR
NICARAGUA
COSTA RICA
PANAMA

BELIZE
HONDURAS
JAMAICA

CUBA

DOMINICAN
REPUBLIC
HAITI

BARBADOS
TRINIDAD AND TOBAGO

VENEZUELA

ECUADOR

COLOMBIA

GUYANA
SURINAM
FRENCH GUIANA

Amazon

EQUATOR

Lima

PERU

BRAZIL

Arica

BOLIVIA

Brasilia

CHILE

ANDES

PARAGUAY

Sao
Paulo

Rio de
Janeiro

Santiago

ARGENTINA

Buenos
Aires

URUGUAY

Falklands

| 0 | miles | 1000 |
| 0 | km | 1000 |

185

70 Central America, Caribbean

The United States helped Cuba to free itself from Spain (1898), got Panama to break away from Colombia, and then built the Panama Canal (1904–14). The 10-mile-wide Panama Canal Zone was garrisoned and controlled by the US, which also obtained a naval base at Guantánamo in Cuba. These and other small ex-Spanish states in the region became, in effect, protectorates of the US, which, until the 1930s, repeatedly sent troops to stop civil wars or restore order. Several of these states (Costa Rica being a notable exception) became notorious for oppressive military or ultra-rightist rule. In 1954 a leftist government in Guatemala was ousted by exiled rightists who, with American support, launched an invasion from Honduras and Nicaragua. In 1965 US forces intervened to stop a civil war in the Dominican Republic; but they were soon replaced by a force provided by other members of the OAS (69), which also withdrew after elections had been held.

The 1956–59 civil war in Cuba ended in victory for the forces led by Fidel Castro, who then imposed a communist regime with support from Russia, on which Cuba became dependent for both economic and military aid. The landing by American-backed Cuban anti-communists at the Bay of Pigs in 1961 was easily repelled. In 1962 the Americans detected Soviet preparations to install in Cuba nuclear missiles aimed at the US. After a tense confrontation, which alarmed the whole world, the Russian ships carrying the missiles to Cuba were turned back (10). However, Soviet aid enabled Cuba to build up strong armed forces. In the 1970s Russian-equipped Cuban forces were sent to fight in Angola and Ethiopia. They were still there in 1982 (34, 35).

The impact of a communist-ruled Cuba on the region has not been the only cause of recent tensions there. An old dispute about the border line between Honduras and El Salvador, and the Hondurans' expulsion of illegal Salvadorean immigrants, led to a war in 1969 – quickly ended by OAS mediation. Guatemala has long pressed claims to Belize (formerly British Honduras). Belize became independent in 1981, after much delay caused by Guatemalan threats to seize it as soon as the British left. As Guatemala did not renounce its claims, Belize got Britain to leave a small force there after independence.

186

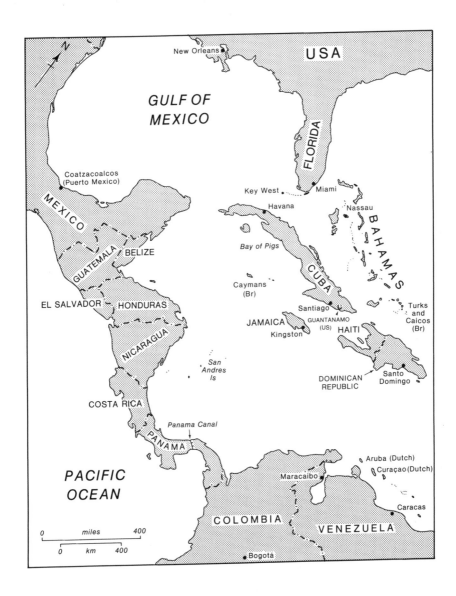

Britain had hoped that its Caribbean colonies could unite on their way to independence. A West Indian Federation was formed in 1958; but Jamaica soon withdrew, and Trinidad followed it. By 1982, 11 ex-British states had become independent separately (9); and there were still several small vestiges of British rule in the region – as well as Dutch and French islands (see also *71*, and for Caricom see *69*).

In Panama, discontent over the terms of the 1903 Canal Treaty led to rioting in 1964, and the US agreed to start new negotiations. Three treaties signed in 1977 came into effect in 1979. The American-run Canal Zone was abolished; Panama took over the ports at each end of the Canal; it obtained more influence in the operation of the Canal itself, and was to take full control of it in the year 2000. An oil pipeline across western Panama, mainly to handle Alaskan oil bound for the eastern US (*67*), was completed in 1982. By then there was also a 'land bridge' for container traffic across Mexico – a modernized railway running from Coatzacoalcos (Puerto Mexico) to the Pacific.

Mexico, Colombia and Venezuela have sought to moderate some of the troubles among the region's smaller states. All three have opposed Guatemala's claims on Belize; Mexico has made particular efforts to improve relations between Cuba and other Latin American states. But Colombia has a dispute of its own with Nicaragua, over the San Andres and neighbouring islets, and it also has a dispute over sea boundaries with Venezuela.

In 1979 in Nicaragua the rule of the Somoza family, who had headed a series of rightist dictatorships since 1936, was ended after a civil war in which the leftist Sandinista guerrillas found widespread support. Once in power, the Sandinista junta lost much of this support by silencing its critics and putting off the elections it had promised. In El Salvador in 1980 several guerrilla groups, mainly communist-led, formed a common front, and civil war developed with the failure of reformers' attempts to replace the old rightist regime with a more democratic one. There were signs that these developments might be leading to a general struggle involving five Central American states. The US accused Nicaragua of smuggling arms from Cuba and Russia into El Salvador (across the Gulf of Fonseca or through thinly peopled Honduras) and also into Costa Rica, Honduras and Guatemala. Nicaragua accused Honduras of helping exile groups which had launched raids into Nicaragua, mainly in the Mosquito Coast area (where many Miskito Indians had fled from Nicaragua into Honduras). The Salvadorean guerrillas had gained control of areas near the Honduran frontier, and in 1982 Honduras moved troops up to the frontier to try to stop the guerrillas using bases in its territory. In Guatemala, too, there was a continuing guerrilla rebellion, partly caused by the army's brutal treatment of restive Indian peasants, which had set off a flight of refugees into Mexico. In the United

States there was anxiety about the risk of deeper American involvement in these conflicts, and specifically about the way the Salvadorean army, which had become heavily dependent on American aid, was carrying out repressive actions that alienated much of the population.

71 East Caribbean, Guianas

In 1962 the West Indian Federation broke up (70), and Trinidad (with Tobago) became independent; in 1966 Barbados followed suit. Britain invited most of its remaining East Caribbean colonies to become 'associated states' – self-governing, with only foreign relations and defence left in British hands, and free to claim independence when they wanted it. Six took up this offer in 1967–69 but, of these, Grenada chose independence in 1974, Dominica in 1978, St Lucia and St Vincent in 1979, Antigua (with Barbuda) in 1981. (The 1000 Barbudans hoped to break away from Antigua, but were dissuaded.) St Kitts–Nevis–Anguilla became an associated state in 1967, but the 6000 Anguillans resisted control from St Kitts and in 1971 Britain resumed responsibility for Anguilla. In December 1982 it was decided that St Kitts (with Nevis) would become independent in 1983.

The East Caribbean map thus shows an array of new sovereign states mingled with the remaining American, British, Dutch and French islands. Puerto Rico is a self-governing 'commonwealth' in free association with the United States. Guadeloupe (with St Barthélemy and part of St Martin) and Martinique are French overseas *départements*, as is also French Guiana (Guyane) on the mainland. Guyana (formerly British Guiana) and Surinam (ex-Dutch Guiana) became independent respectively in 1966 and 1975.

A disturbing dispute arose from Venezuela's claim to more than half of Guyana – the whole area west of the Essequibo river. In 1982 an agreement by which the dispute had been set aside for 12 years expired. Tension increased, Guyana accused Venezuela of violating the frontier, and both states sought support from other countries. Racial divisions have troubled Guyana; the ancestors of about half of its people came from Africa, half from India. Similar divisions exist in Surinam, and a third of its population have migrated to Holland in recent years; its elected government was ousted in 1980 by a military coup, and in December 1982 the soldiers' repressive actions led Holland to suspend the economic aid on which Surinam was still heavily dependent.

A coup in Grenada in 1979 installed a leftist regime whose links with Cuba and failure to hold promised elections aroused concern both in the

US and among the other ex-British island states, which had been able to hold regular and free elections and maintain democratic practices and rights. However, in 1982 Grenada was still a member of Caricom (69).

72 Argentina

In 1982 Argentina's armed forces seized the Falklands and South Georgia. Ten weeks later the occupying troops surrendered to the counter-attacking British; but the conflict, and its repercussions, brought Argentina worldwide attention.

Compared with most other Latin American countries, Argentina has a high national income per head. It has a large temperate zone, vast fertile plains, oil, gas, uranium (3, 4) and other mineral resources, extensive industries and good communications. Its population – about 28 million – is mainly of European origin and has not grown disastrously fast (1); after 170 years of independence, it is not at all a typical 'third-world' country. Yet its production and living standards are far lower than those of, e.g., Canada – which has comparable resources and population and a more severe climate.

Geography has shielded Argentina from external threats. But it has maintained large armed forces, which have carried out many coups (e.g. in 1930, 1943, 1955, 1966 and 1976) and have influenced politics even when not openly holding power. It has often been able to dominate its smaller neighbours – including, at times, Chile, on the other side of the Andes mountains. Military regimes in Bolivia and Paraguay have had support from Buenos Aires, whose influence has sometimes reached much farther north.

In recent years expansionist ideas in Argentina have also been turned towards the south. After the exploiting of oilfields in previously undeveloped Patagonia, hopes of offshore oil have increased interest in the waters around Cape Horn, the Falklands and other southern islands, and the Antarctic continent. Like other signatories of the 1959 Antarctic Treaty (12), Argentina has agreed not to press its claims south of 60° South for the time being, but some of its actions have shown that it wants to strengthen those claims with an eye to the future.

The introduction of 200-mile sea zones (6) has intensified Argentina's old quarrel with Chile over the three small islands, Lennox, Nueva and Picton, at the eastern end of the Beagle Channel, south of Tierra del Fuego (73), because possession of these islands could now determine the control of large adjacent areas of sea. In 1971 both governments agreed to

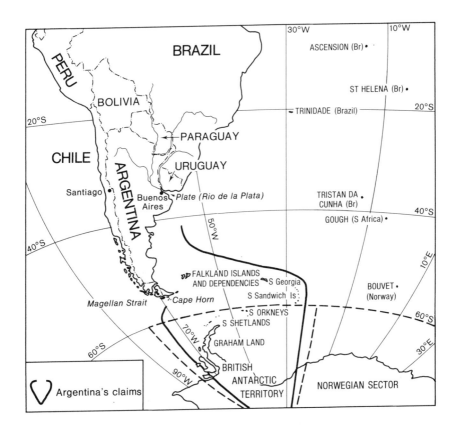

accept arbitration of the dispute. The decision given by five judges of the International Court in 1977 favoured Chile. Argentina rejected it and seemed about to go to war; but after some tense months it agreed to refer the case to the Pope. The Pope's proposals, presented in 1980, were accepted by Chile but not by Argentina. In 1982 many Chileans expected that, if Argentina's invasion of the Falklands and South Georgia was a success, it would attempt a similar move against the Beagle Channel islands.

73 Falklands

The Falkland Islands (in Spanish, Malvinas) were uninhabited until settlements were established by the French (1764), the British (1765) and the Spanish (1767). The French renounced their claims and left; Britain withdrew its garrison in 1774 but maintained its claims; Spain maintained a garrison and a convict station until 1810; the islands were then abandoned, although American, British and French sealing ships visited them. Argentina asserted a claim to the islands in the 1820s but failed to establish effective control. Britain reasserted its claims, effectively, in 1833, and by the 1850s the British colony was doing well, with sheep farming expanding and Port Stanley servicing ships on voyages around Cape Horn. Later, Port Stanley lost business when steamships, using the Magellan Strait, found Punta Arenas in Chile a more convenient port of call; but wool production continued to support a population of about 2000 on the Falklands. (There was no permanent settlement on any of their Dependencies, although from 1904 on whaling stations were built in South Georgia – 72.)

Argentina maintained its claims, and found much support in Latin America for its 'anti-colonial' arguments, despite the Falklanders' British origin and their strong wish to remain under British protection. In 1965 Britain and Argentina began to hold talks, in which Britain – having promised the islanders that sovereignty would not be transferred without their consent – tried to concentrate on plans for economic co-operation; but in 1977 it agreed to discuss the question of sovereignty too. Argentina stepped up its pressure, and uncertainty about the future discouraged investment in the Falklands and contributed to a decline in their population to about 1800.

In April 1982 Argentina suddenly interrupted the talks by occupying the Falklands and South Georgia, landing about 14,000 soldiers on the islands. An incident provoked by a group of Argentines who raised an Argentine flag in South Georgia served as a pretext for the invasion; but its timing was determined by the Argentine military regime's urgent need for a diversion from its mounting domestic difficulties.

The British tried to negotiate an Argentine withdrawal but, when American and other diplomatic initiatives had failed, they made a

successful counter-attack. A British force was landed in the north-west of
East Falkland which, after 25 days of fighting on land, recaptured Port
Stanley and obliged all the Argentine troops in the islands to surrender on
14 June. (South Georgia had been recaptured in late April.) Argentine
aircraft flying from mainland bases inflicted serious losses on the British
forces, which were operating at extreme range – Ascension Island, 3400
miles from the Falklands (72), having the nearest airfield and staging
point available to them.

After the surrender, Argentina gave no firm assurance that it would not
attack the Falklands again. Britain seemed to face a costly and hazardous
task in providing defences for the islands.

Index

Each number refers to a map and the accompanying notes, not to a page. A number in **bold** type indicates a more detailed reference. Words in capital letters are acronyms or abbreviations. 'Fo.' = formerly.

Baluchs, Baluchistan, 47, 49–51
Bamako, 36
Banaba (Ocean Island), 65
Bandar Khomeini (fo. Bandar Shahpur), 46
Bandung, 27, 63
Bangkok, 60, 61
Bangladesh, 1, 9, 28, 51, 52
Bangui, 32, 37
Banjul (fo. Bathurst), 36
'Bantustans', 33
Barbados, 9, 71
Barbary: see Berber
Barbuda, 71
Barcelona, 23
Barents Sea, 22
Barotseland, 32
Basotho Qwa Qwa, 33
Basques, 23
Basra, 45–48
Basutoland: see Lesotho
Bataan, 62
Batan, 55
Batavia: see Jakarta
Bathurst: see Banjul
Battambang, 60, 61
Bauxite, 5
Bavaria (Bayern), 18
Bay of Pigs, 70
Bayern: see Bavaria
Baykonur: see Baikonur
Beagle Channel, 72, 73
Bear Island, 22
Beaufort Sea, 11, 68
Bechar, 38, 39
Bechuanaland: see Botswana
Beersheba, 42, 43
Beijing (Peking), 53, 54
Beira, 32
Beirut, 42, 43, 44
Bejaia (fo. Bougie), 38
Bekaa, 44
Belfast, 24
Belgian Congo: see Zaire

Belgium, 12, 19, 20, 22, 23, 27, 32, 35
Belgrade, 7, 13, 17
Belize (fo. British Honduras), 8, 9, 70
Belmopan, 70
Benelux, 19
Bengal, 50, 51
Benghazi, 38
Benguela, 32–34
Benin (fo. Dahomey), 30, 36, 37
Benin City, 36
Berber, 38
Berbera, 35
Bering Strait, 11, 15, 67
Berlin, 8, 13, 16, 18, 20
Bermuda, 9, 69
Berne, 23
Bessarabia, 14
Bethlehem, 43
Bhutan, 51, 52
Biafra, 36
Biarritz, 23
Bihar, 51
Bikini, 10, 66
Bilbao, 23
BIOT, 9, 41
Birobijan, 53
'Boat people', 59
Bokhara (Bukhara), 49, 53
Bolivia, 5, 69, 72
Bolzano (Bozen), 23
Bombay, 51
Bonaire, 71
Bone: see Annaba
Bonins (Ogasawara), 57, 66
Bonn, 18
Bophuthatswana, 33
Borneo (Kalimantan), 8, 59, 62, 63
Bornholm, 21
Bosnia, 17
Bosphorus, 6
Botswana (fo. Bechuanaland), 9, 30–34

Bou Craa, 39
Bougainville, 63
Bougie: see Bejaia
Bouvet, 12
Bozen: see Bolzano
Brahmaputra, 51
Brasilia, 69
Bratsk, 53
Brazil, 1, 3–5, 69, 72
Brazzaville, 32, 37
Bremen, 18
Brest-Litovsk, 14
Bretons: see Brittany
Brisbane, 64
Britain (United Kingdom), 1–13, 18–27, 31–36, 40–42, 45–47, 50, 52, 56–59, 62, 65, 69–73
British Antarctic Territory, 12, 72, 73
British Columbia, 68
British Honduras: see Belize
British Indian Ocean Territory, 9, 41
British North Borneo: see Sabah
British Virgins, 71
Brittany, 23
Brunei, 3, 9, 54, 62, 63
Brunswick, 18
Brussels, 19, 20
Bucharest, 16
Budapest, 16
Buenos Aires, 69, 72
Buganda, 35
Bujumbura (fo. Usumbura), 35
Bukavu, 32
Bukovina, 14
Bulawayo, 32
Bulgaria, 13, 16, 17
Bunyoro, 35
Buraimi, 46
Burma, 9, 41, 52, 54, 57, 59
Burundi, 8, 30, 35

Byelorussia, 8, 14, 15

Cabinda, 34
Cabora Bassa, 32
Cadiz, 25
Caicos, 70
Cairo, 29, 40
Calcutta, 51, 52
Calgary, 68
California, 67
Cambodia (Kampuchea),
  8, 54, 59, 60, 61, 62
Cameroons (Cameroun),
  8, 30, 36, 37
Camp David, 43
Camranh, 60
Canada, 1–5, 7–11, 19,
  20, 67, 68
Canberra, 64
Canton (Guangzhou), 56
Cape Horn, 66, 69, 72, 73
Cape of Good Hope, 33,
  40
Cape Province, 33
Cape Town, 33
Cape Verde Islands 36
Caprivi Strip, 34
CAR: see Central African
  Republic
Caracas, 69, 70
Cardamon Mts, 61
Caribbean, 6, 70, 71
Caricom, 69, 71
Carolines, 57, 66
Carpathians, 17
Casablanca, 39
Catalonia, 23
Caucasus, 15, 47
Cayenne, 71
Caymans, 9, 70
Celebes (Sulawesi), 63
Celtic Sea, 22
CENTO, 45
Central African
  Federation, 31
Central African Republic
  (fo. Ubangui-Chari),
  30, 37

Central Asia, 15, 28, 47,
  53
Ceram: see Seram
Ceuta, 25, 29, 39
Ceylon: see Sri Lanka
Chad, 30, 35, 36, 37
Chagos, 41
Chandernagore, 50
Channel Islands, 22, 23
Cheju (Quelpart), 58
Chekiang: see Zhejiang
Chemnitz: see Karl-Marx-
  Stadt
Chenpao: see Damansky
Chile, 5, 12, 69, 72, 73
Chin, 52
China, 1–8, 10, 17, 27,
  28, 32, 49–52, 53–56,
  57–61
Chinese, 'overseas', 59–63
Chios, 26
Chita, 53
Chittagong, 51
Chongqing (Chungking),
  54
Christchurch, 64
Christmas Island, 10
Chrome, 5
Chungking: see
  Chongqing
Ciskei, 33
Ciudad Bolivar (fo.
  Angostura), 71
Ciudad Trujillo: see
  Santo Domingo
Cluj, 17
CMEA (Comecon), 13
Coal, 2, 15, 64, 67
Cobalt, 5
Cologne (Köln), 18
Colomb Bechar, 38
Colombia, 3, 69, 70
Colombo, 51
Comecon (CMEA), 13
Common Market: see
  EEC
Commonwealth, 9
Comoros, 41

Congo, 30–32, 37 (see
  also Zaire)
Constantine: see
  Qacentina
Constantinople: see
  Istanbul
Cook Islands, 64, 65
Copenhagen, 21
Copper, 5, 31, 32
Copts, 28
Coquilhatville: see
  Mbandaka
Cordoba, 25
Corfu, 17
Cork, 24
Corsica, 23
Cos, 26
Costa Rica, 70
Cracow (Krakow), 16
Craigavon, 24
Crete, 26
Crimea, 15
Croatia, 17
CSCE, 13
Cuando, 34
Cuba, 5, 7, 8, 10, 69, 70
Cuban forces in Africa,
  34, 35
Cubango, 34
Cunene, 34
Curaçao, 70, 71
Cyprus, 8, 9, 20, 26
Cyrenaica, 38
Czechoslovakia, 8, 13, 14,
  16, 18, 20

Dacca (Dhaka), 50–52
Dahomey: see Benin
Dairen: see Lüda
Dakar, 36, 39
Dakhla (fo. Villa
  Cisneros), 39
Dalat, 60
Dallas, 67
Daman, 50
Damansky (Chenpao), 53
Damara, 34
Damascus, 42–44

Kuwait, 3, 8, 29, 40, 45, 46, 48
Kuzbas, 53
Kwajalein, 66
Kwangju, 58
Kwangsi: see Guangxi
Kwangtung: see Guangdong
KwaZulu, 33
Kweichow: see Guizhou
Kyongsong: see Seoul
Kyrenia, 26

Labrador, 68
Ladakh, 52
Lae, 63
LAFTA, 69
Lagos, 36
Lahore, 50
LAIA, 69
Lakshadweep (Laccadive islands), 50, 51
La Linea, 25
Languedoc, 23
Laos, 54, 59, 60, 61
Larnaca, 26
Latvia, 14, 21
Lebanon, 8, 29, 42, 43, 44
Lebowa, 33
Leh, 52
Leipzig, 18
Lemnos, 26
Lena, 15
Leningrad, 14, 15, 21
Leninsk, 53
Lennox, 73
Leopoldville: see Kinshasa
Lesbos, 26
Lesotho (fo. Basutoland), 9, 30, 33
Lhasa, 52
Liberia, 27, 36
Libya, 3, 8, 28–30, 35, 37, 38, 40
Liechtenstein, 23
Lilongwe, 32

Limassol, 26
Limerick, 24
Limpopo, 32
Litani, 44
Lithuania, 14, 21
Lobito, 32
Lod (Lydda), 43
Lomé, 19, 36
Londonderry, 24
Lop Nor, 10, 53
Lourenço Marques: see Maputo
Lower Saxony (Niedersachsen), 18
Luanda, 32, 34
Luang Prabang, 60
Lubango (fo. Sa da Bandeira), 34
Lubeck, 18
Lublin, 16
Lubumbashi (fo. Elisabethville), 32
Lüda (fo. Dairen and Port Arthur), 53
Lüderitz, 34
Luluabourg: see Kananga
Lusaka, 32
Lusatia, 18
Lushai Hills: see Mizoram
Lu-Ta: see Lüda
Luxembourg, 19, 20, 23
Lydda: see Lod

Macao, 56
Macassar (Ujung Pandang), 63
Macedonia, 17
Macias Nguema: see Fernando Poo
Mackenzie, 11, 68
McMahon Line, 52
Madagascar (fo. Malagasy), 30, 41
Madhya Pradesh, 51
Madras, 51
Magadan, 11, 15
Magdeburg, 18
Magellan Strait, 6, 72, 73

Maghreb, 39
Maharashtra, 51
Malacca Strait, 6, 62
Malaga, 25
Malagasy: see Madagascar
Malawi (fo. Nyasaland), 31, 32
Malaya, 57, 62
Malayalam, 51
Malaysia, 3, 5, 9, 28, 41, 54, 59, 62, 63
Maldives, 9, 41
Mali (fo. Soudan), 30, 36, 37
Malta, 8, 9, 25, 38, 41
Maluku (Moluccas), 63
Malvinas: see Falklands
Managua, 70
Manchuria, 53, 57, 58
Mandalay, 52
Manganese, 5, 6
Manila, 59, 62
Manipur, 51
Manitoba, 68
Maputo (fo. Lourenço Marques), 32
Maracaibo, 70
Marathi, 51
Marianas, 57, 66
Maritimes, 68
Marjayoun, 44
Maronites, 28, 44
Marrakesh, 39
Marshall Plan, 19
Marshalls, 10, 57, 66
Martinique, 71
Mary (Merv), 49
Mashona, 32
Masira, 41, 45
Massawa, 35
Matabele, 32, 33
Matsu, 55
Mauritania, 29, 30, 37, 39
Mauritius, 9, 30, 41
Mayotte, 41
Mbandaka (fo. Coquilhatville), 32
Mecca, 28, 29, 45